BATTLES, BU~~LL~~
&
MAYHEM !

Devon's Turbulent Past

by

Grahame Holloway

Acknowledgements

My grateful thanks go out to many people, too many to mention
individually, who went out of their way to provide information for
this book. These include the staff at the West Country Study Centre,
the Archivist at Powderham Castle, farmers who permitted me onto
their land and the many kind people who invited me into their homes
to share their knowledge of local history.   I am also indebted to
Dr. Leo Baker for his editing of the final draft.

****

For

Jessica, Samuel, Jamie and Thomas

****

First published 2001

by

BREVET 2000

3 Parkers Cross Lane, Pinhoe, Exeter, EX1 3TA

Printed in Great Britain

By

Grant Turner Imprint, 2 Church Court, St. James Street,
Okehampton, Devon, EX20 1DJ

Copyright: Grahame Holloway

ISBN 0-9539015-1-3

Contents   *Page*

INTRODUCTION

Today television can bring pictures from around the world into one's home within moments. Horrific scenes of carnage caused by terrorism in the United States can quickly switch to unrest in Asia or riots in Europe. Compared to many of these events Great Britain seems almost an idyllic spot. Yet here, too, we have experienced more than our share of violence through the centuries. From the warring tribes of the pre-Roman era, the Pax Romana was in turn followed by Danish raids, the Norman invasion, Wars of the Roses, the Prayer Book Rebellion, the Civil War and so on. Even in comparatively more recent times we have endured industrial, religious and political riots. But not here in Devon, one might say. Wrong ! Devon has suffered as much as anywhere else.

In **"Battles, Bullets & Mayhem"** local writer **Grahame Holloway** takes a glimpse at some of the more violent events to have occurred in **Devon** over the past two thousand years. As a former senior police officer in the Devon & Cornwall Constabulary, he has a personal interest in both social unrest and local history.

"Battles, Bullets & Mayhem" is by no means intended to be a definitive history book although in places some of the events described have come direct from published contemporary reports. The author looks at it more as a local guide informing the reader of Devon's unruly past and perhaps making one glad to live in the present. Many of the locations featured within its pages can be still visited in moments of leisure and most will be easily accessible. However, where they are now on private land this will be stated and the owners' privacy should be respected.

Chapter One

DUMNONII, ROMANS & SAXONS

The PRE-ROMAN ERA

If a time machine could take us back over two thousand years we would discover a Devon where Celtic tribes lived in small societies, often with a local *'king'* as their head. Hill forts were used to protect their lands and many of these still remain. Their weapons comprised axes, swords and spears, examples of which may now be seen in local museums.

One of Devon's oldest settlements is the early fortified Bronze Age village of Grimspound which can be found on Dartmoor at O.S. Map 191/701809. Here the remains of some two dozen hut circles are clearly visible within their protective enclosure.

In East Devon the local tribe, the Dumnonii, looked upon the valley of the Axe as their eastern frontier beyond which were the Durotriges whose territory was present day Dorset. Although we have very little real evidence, it is almost certain there was occasional conflict between the tribes, the existence of the early iron age hill forts guarding the river valley providing some proof of this.

Two examples, strategically placed on high ground, can still be found at Hawksdown Hill and also above Musbury. Those interested in locating the sites will find the former marked at O.S. Map 193/263914 whilst the latter is at 193/282942. Further inland and to the West another fine example of an early iron-age settlement can be found at Hembury Fort, situated on the highest point between Honiton and Cullompton and lying just north of the A373. (O.S. Map 193/113030). Over a thousand feet in length, its approach is steep, being a factor it relied on for its defence. This should, however, not be confused with the similarly named Hembury Castle, a hill-fort of similar age which lies a couple of miles north of Buckfastleigh and is easily accessible.

Other easily accessible examples can still be seen at Blackbury Camp, near Beer, and at Woodbury Castle. The latter occupies a fine vantage point, with views towards the coast and the Exe, about five miles south east of Exeter. Both sites still have their defensive ditches dating from around the second century BC. Of these Blackbury Camp is perhaps the most interesting as it is now scheduled as an Ancient Monument and in the care of English Heritage. It is well signed from the A3052 Exeter to Lyme Regis road and will be found at map ref. O.S. Map 193/187923.

There is limited car parking at the site. An information board at its entrance describes the site's history and indicates evidence of occupation at least two hundred years before the arrival of the Romans. It also shows the layout of the camp, the detail of which is reproduced opposite.

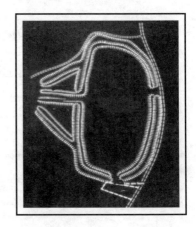

The Romans

The lives of these ancient Britons were to change forever when Rome commenced its invasion of Britain in 43 AD with legions under Alus Platinus landing in the South East of England. However, this was not their only point of disembarkation for there was soon a need for them to open supply facilities along the channel coast and one of the suitable anchorages they found for this purpose was at Axmouth in Devon.

It was perhaps inevitable, given the size and strength of the Roman army, that eventually all resistance would be overcome and gradually Roman rule spread over much of the country. Only the fringe Celtic kingdoms of what are today Scotland, Wales and Cornwall remained free.

Whilst we know the local Dumnonii were a strong people, there is little hard evidence to pinpoint battles between them and the invading Romans although undoubtedly there was some resistance. In *Celtic Britain* by John Rhys , for example, reference is made to the fact that the Roman general, Vespasian, engaged the enemy on no fewer than thirty occasions and that one of the most powerful peoples he subdued were the *Dumnonii*. Unfortunately any points of conflict between the Dumnonii and the Romans were not recorded although it is probable the hill-forts at Hawkesdown and Musbury presented at least some resistance. We do know that in the end the local tribes were militarily no match for the disciplined Roman legions.

Seaton became an important Roman staging post although any evidence of their presence disappeared long ago. Not so, however, twenty-five miles away at Exeter which was to become their furthest garrison to the west. Beyond lay inhospitable Dartmoor and the Celtic tribes. At first Exeter was purely a military outpost where basic accommodation for the Legion was protected by earth ramparts and wooden stockade with the River Exe providing a natural barrier on its western flank. The Romans called their garrison *Isca Dumnoniorum* after the river and the local Dumnonii.

As Roman influence grew across the land and their law prevailed, so their early garrisons grew into prosperous towns of which one of the more prominent was *Isca Dumnoniorum*. As it expanded so the early stockade was removed to be replaced by strong walls encompassing a far greater area within which a sizable and prosperous city grew. It was a period of peace, the *Pax Romana*, and it was to last for over three hundred years.

Fortunately, evidence of *Isca Dumnoniorum* still exists within the present day city of Exeter. There are some fine stretches of the ancient Roman wall and these are clearly visible for those who take the time to search them out. Here a good city street plan will prove invaluable but for those without one the longest and arguably the best section will be found running behind Southernhay West.

This stretches from South Street, along the side of the Southgate Hotel, to end with the ruins of a watch tower a few yards from Paris Street. Another substantial section will be found in Northernhay Gardens, again close to the city centre. However, they are not all original for like so many fortifications they were added to and improved by later generations, not least by the Normans.

Part of the City Wall near the Southgate Hotel

Sadly, what is perhaps Exeter's finest relic of the Roman era, a fine bath house which was probably part of the military garrison, is currently lost to public view. Reputedly one of the best in Britain, it lies in front of the west door of Exeter Cathedral, having been excavated between 1971-76. However, being so close to the cathedral gave rise to a number of problems, not least one of preservation. In the end the site was re-covered in sand to ensure that if a future generation wishes to re-excavate it at least their task will be made easy. Luckily, other evidence has been preserved and can be seen at the Royal Albert Memorial Museum in Queen Street.

Another part of the Roman wall
will be found near the end of Princesshay

Whilst Britain enjoyed a long period of peace all was not well for the Romans at home. In 383 AD Magnus Maximum withdrew most of his forces from Britain to fight a campaign in Europe only to be defeated and killed five years later in battle close to home in Northern Italy. The death of Emperor Theodosis in 395 AD saw the beginnings of a split in the Roman Empire and a decade later Constantine III virtually withdrew the last of his troops from Britain to back his claims to a unified Rome. These were unsuccessful and in 410 AD Rome was sacked by the Goths. In the face of such domestic problems Emperor Honorius finally told his British colony that from now on they would have to stand alone and be responsible for their own defence.

The Saxons

The departure of the Roman legions was to herald a dark age for Britain and the 5th Century once again saw Britain subject to invasion. This time the invaders were the Germanic tribes, the most prominent of which were the Angles and Saxons. The Angles, migrating from Southern Denmark, tended to colonise the eastern side of Britain and even today we continue to refer to this part of the country as East Anglia. The Saxons on the other hand moved westwards and by the 6th Century had reached the lands of the Dumnonii, by then largely accustomed to the Roman way of life. At first there was wide-scale resistance to the Saxons throughout the country although the indigenous population was soon overcome in a series of decisive battles. One such battle reputedly took place in 612 AD when the Dumnonii and Saxons fought above the Axe Valley, the locals probably defending their hill forts. The Dumnonii suffered heavy casualties and the Saxon advance continued.

By the 8th Century the Saxons prevailed in the West and had established the Kingdom of Wessex. Again there was a period of stability as Saxon law prevailed. Towns grew up and early Christian churches were built. In Wessex there was a succession of Kings who were to become household names, the best known of these undoubtedly being Alfred the Great. Even so, like the rest of England, Devon was not completely at peace. Saxon settlements close to the coast were frequently the target for raids by large bands of Danes intent on pillage, plunder and rape.

'The King's England' records that Crediton had "...*a Saxon cathedral and nine Saxon bishops before the see was transferred to Exeter to be out of the way of the Vikings...*" and Devon County Council lists records of all known battle sites although in many instances further information is rather scarce. Amongst battles listed are Slapton in AD 835 and Wicganbeorg in AD 851. This latter battle was fought close to the East Devon village of Wiggaton, near Ottery St Mary. However, perhaps one of the most famous was the 'Battle of Bloody Corner' which is covered in some detail next.

Kenwith Castle and the Battle of Bloody Corner

In the 9th Century one of the Saxon strongholds was Kenwith Castle, a typical hill-fort situated close to the North Devon coast and near the present town of Northam. Marked at map ref. 180/433274, traces of its defensive 'motte' have survived but are now located within the private grounds of 'Kenwith Castle', a large residential care home for the elderly. However, it is not completely hidden from view and can be seen from the viaduct carrying the A39 across the Kenwith Valley. It is the tree-topped mound close to the ornamental lake in the grounds of the nursing home.

From contemporary stories it appears that the first sign of trouble was when local lookouts spotted a large fleet of ships sailing into Bideford Bay. The number of vessels varies according to the source but the local authority's tablet at Bone Hill puts the number at thirty-three. It was also to transpire that these carried a Danish invasion force of over a thousand men led by King Hubba. Where the army landed is not sure but would certainly have been in the area of the Torridge estuary, probably near Appledore.

Outnumbered, the local Saxons initially retreated to the relative safety of Kenwith Castle from where, reinforced and with spirits raised, they emerged once more to meet the might of the Danish army. Local folklore says they were led by King Alfred in person whilst others say he was not there at all. What is certain is that their leader sufficiently inspired them to win a decisive battle during which over eight hundred of the Danish invasion force were slain and amongst them was King Hubba. Those who fell were later buried nearby at a spot known today as Bone Hill.

Bone Hill is worth a visit for two reasons. Firstly, there is the historic context but secondly there are also excellent views from there. These extend across Bideford Bay and seawards as far as the distant island of Lundy. The site is an easy two-minute stroll along Tower Street from Northam's square or, alternatively, a short walk through the churchyard from the town's large free car park.

The tablet installed there reads as follows:

> *"An invasion force of thirty-three ships, led by Danish King Hubba,*
> *is said to have landed at Appledore in 878. The Danes were*
> *vanquished at Bloody Corner in Northam by an English force led by*
> *King Alfred and many of the invaders are believed to be buried under*
> *this very spot of Bone Hill."*

The tablet then explains that 'Bone Hill' is derived from the Anglo Saxon word 'Bunhill', meaning 'burial ground.'

Today 'Bloody Corner' is marked by a roadside tablet on the outskirts of Northam, its exact spot being on the right hand side of an acute bend on the main road to Appledore, (O.S. Map 180/454292). The granite stone is set behind railings and beseeches one to stop with the inscription:

> *"STOP STRANGER, STOP,*
> *NEAR THIS SPOT LIES BURIED*
> *KING HUBBA THE DANE,*
> *WHO WAS SLAIN BY ALFRED THE GREAT*
> *IN BLOODY RETREAT."*

Bone Hill. Northam

The date recorded on the stone is given as AD 892 which conflicts with county records showing it as AD 878. Such discrepancies often arise due to the fact that they were not recorded in writing until a century or more later when the stories, passed by word of mouth, became distorted. There is no doubt, however, that around these dates a mighty battle was fought here.

Alfred had acceded to the throne in 871 AD and was to rule for the next twenty-eight years during which Wessex was to become the dominant British kingdom. On his death his son, Edward the Elder, ruled until 924 AD when he was succeeded by Athelstan, Alfred the Great's grandson. His accession was to open a new chapter in our history for it was Athelstan who is credited with uniting Britain as one Kingdom.

By the mid-ninth century Britain was still a divided country and it is said that the turning point came with the *Battle of Brunanburh* in 937 AD. That the battle took place, there is little doubt. Where it took place is, sadly, open to debate. One school of thought puts it somewhere in the North of England, probably Northumbria, whilst another sets it in the Axe Valley of Devon. Each submit a convincing argument, the former saying that as Athelstan's enemies were the Viking kingdoms to the North and East it was only natural that he would go forth to meet them.

Conversely, it can be argued that the Vikings, being great seafarers, would think nothing of sailing around the coast of England to mount an attack on Athelstan's kingdom to further their own territorial expansion.

The Battle of Brunanburh

Here we look at the evidence for placing the battle in Devon and commence with the indisputable evidence that, for at least five centuries before it was fought, the Vikings and Danes frequently raided the Devon coast. In fact one ancient chronicler wrote that the Danes were led by Anlaf during a great battle which took place near Musbury in the Axe Valley.

But better evidence, and perhaps the answer, was to be found at Newenham Abbey which once flourished close to the banks of the Axe about a mile south west of Axminster. Only scant remains of the abbey are to be found today but one of its early records is said to have included the following words.

> *"King Athelstan gave the church of Axminster to seven priests*
> *who should there forever serve god, for the souls of seven earls*
> *and many others put to death in battle with him against foreign*
> *invaders, which fight began at Calix Down, in the Parish of Colyton,*
> *and extended to Colecroft below Axminster."*

This description would put the battle in the broad valley of the River Axe which, unlike today, was then navigable by both sailing boats and Viking longboats. It is also interesting that an ancient poem from an Anglo-Saxon Chronicle relates a battle ...

> *"... How blood flowed on that fateful day from the rise of the sun ... Five Viking kings were put asleep and seven strong earls ..."*

One can only surmise that this record was transferred from the church to the abbey at a much later date, probably after the original Saxon church was replaced by the Normans, for the abbey was not built until the early thirteenth century. Its founder, Reginald de Mohun, was reputedly laid to rest in front of the altar in 1257.

Whilst doubts may still linger in some minds as to whether this was the actual site of the Battle of Brunanburh there is no doubt that historians can agree that King Athelstan did indeed fight a great battle here in the Axe Valley. To view what would probably have been the site of Athelstan's great victory one has only to drive along the A358 as it follows the eastern bank of the river between Seaton and Axminster.

The Axe Valley as it is today

Of Newenham Abbey only a few fragments remain and these lie within the curtilage of a private farm reached by a narrow lane from the appropriately named Abbey Gate crossroads. Permission would be needed for viewing but it is hardly worth the trouble. Only the outline of a gateway and a short section of wall can seen and even these have been incorporated into the interior of a barn and cannot be seen from the outside.

Greater reward can be found by visiting Exeter where there are a number of reminders of Athelstan's reign. The great Norman cathedral, of which the city is justly very proud, is reputed to have been built on the site of an earlier Saxon monastery founded by Athelstan when Exeter was already the area's principal town. Much of the Roman wall built to fortify the city had stood the test of time over the centuries and it would have been quite natural for Athelstan to have built further on these defences.

Athelstan's Tower - part of the City Wall in Exeter's Northernhay Gardens

Elsewhere in the city there is an Athelstan Road, reputedly near where he built a dyke as a further defensive measure. Unfortunately he did not enjoy the fruits of his victory in the Axe Valley for long and died two years later.

In the thirty-two years following Athelstan's death there were no fewer than five Saxon kings before Ethelred II, also known as Ethelred the Unready, came to the throne. Although now unified, England nevertheless still suffered attacks from marauding Danes for whom, with their longships, distance seemed no problem. Ethelred was in the twenty-second year of his reign and the new millennium was scarcely a year old when, once again, East Devon was to be subjected to a telling battle between the local Saxons and an invading Danish army.

The Battle of Pinhoe, 1001 AD

This is a battle which has been part of local folklore for centuries. It is the story of the Danes sailing up the River Exe with the intention of sacking the Saxon settlement at Exeter. However, when this attack failed their attention turned to the surrounding countryside. A Saxon army gathered to meet the invaders and eventually the two sides met on the slopes of what is now Church Hill at Pinhoe. Today the battle is recalled in the names given to roads close to the battleground, Danesway and Saxon Avenue being the prime examples. However, the event is not remembered so much for its outcome but rather the actions of the parish priest.

A modern nameplate acts as a battle reminder

The story told is that the battle was going against King Ethelred's army whose Saxon archers were finding themselves short of arrows. Learning of their predicament the priest volunteered to take his donkey through the battle lines to nearby Exeter which, being well defended had repulsed the Danes, and there load his donkey with a fresh supply of arrows for the Saxon bowmen.

So who won? Some reports say it was the Danes but the resultant folklore suggests it may have been otherwise. Following the battle it is said the king awarded the Priest of Pinhoe the sum of one Saxon mark each year which was to be paid in perpetuity. It was a generous reward in those days and one unlikely to have been paid had the battle been lost.

Why one mark? One school of thought says in 1001 this was sufficient money to feed a donkey for one year so in some ways it was a reward for the part played by the donkey as much as the priest. In fairness it must also be said that the reason for the reward is open to some doubt as others suggest it was a payment for prayers to be said regularly for souls of those who fell in the battle, a practice which was common in those days.

Fact or fiction? For a probable answer we turn to a 1930's copy of 'The King's England'. It is accepted by many as a guide of some merit and in its pages is recorded the following fact:

'...for more than 900 years this tribute has been paid and the word of Ethelred is still fulfilled by the British Treasury which, through the Ecclesiastical Commissioners, under the National Debt Act, pays to the vicar of Pinhoe each year the sum of 13s 2d, something apparently having been deducted for expenses."

A much later incumbent confirmed the sum continued to be paid until the mid-20th century when it apparently stopped. By then, however, it was not the local vicar who saw the money for it had become a purely a paper transaction between the Treasury and the Church Commissioners.

Like most legends there is a blurred area as records of the payment did not appear until much later and as a result some say it must have been paid for some other reason although unable to say why. We know, however, that often early events were not recorded in writing at the time but merely passed by word of mouth to be written much later.

Pinhoe Parish Church

Situated high on a hillside, visitors to the church can obtain views of the Exe Estuary and towards the open sea. Those who adopt a more romantic attitude to our history should rest easily with the story of the Pinhoe priest and his donkey for it has been part of local folklore for so long it must be true. Indeed in the summer of 2001 the village held a 'Viking Festival' to celebrate the battle's one thousandth anniversary on its site adjacent to the parish church.

And if still not convinced of the story one can always look at the board outside of the village school and study its coat of arms. There, incorporated within the heraldic design, is a sheath of arrows. Evidence indeed of events !

Pinhoe School's Coat of Arms

Following the death of Ethelred in 1016 the throne of England passed through a succession of monarchs until, in January 1066, it was entrusted to Harold II. What happened in the autumn of that year is probably one of the best documented events of our early history .... the Battle of Hastings and the Norman invasion led by William of Normandy. The era of Saxon independence was over and another chapter in our history was about to unfold.

Chapter Two

FROM NORMANS TO PLANTAGENETS

The Normans

Following the Norman invasion of 1066 their rule prevailed throughout England and William of Normandy reigned as King William I, perhaps better known as 'William the Conqueror'. There was sporadic resistance throughout the land and it is said that Exeter only fell to the Normans in 1068 after a siege. As the conquest continued so Saxon lands were granted to Norman overlords or barons. Great castles sprang up across the English countryside as they increased their grip on the Saxon population and brought in their own code of feudal law.

Amongst those castles erected in Devon were the strongholds at Exeter, Okehampton, Totnes and Plympton. The ruins of all these can still be seen today with those at Okehampton and Totnes being cared for by English Heritage and of sufficient interest for them to be opened to the public.

Whilst reputedly some were never to see any action this was not so in the case of Exeter's Rougemont Castle which was built by Baldwin, a Norman lord appointed by William, soon after the city fell. However, one has to wait almost another seventy years for the story to unfold and, even then, it could be said to be the story of two castles and their part in the barons' uprising.

When William died in 1087 his successor was his eldest son, William Rufus, who reigned as William II. Reputedly a poor monarch, he met an untimely death in 1100 through a suspicious accident whilst hunting in the New Forest. William Rufus was, however, without issue so the throne then passed to the Conqueror's youngest son, Henry I, who reigned well until his death in 1135. Unfortunately, when he died he left no son, only a daughter Matilda. This was a testing time for England. There had never previously been a queen on the throne and Stephen, Count of Blois, seizing his chance usurped the crown from Matilda for himself, reigning as Stephen I.

It was a move which was not universally popular for Matilda was well liked and Stephen's reign was marked by spasmodic civil wars and anarchy. However, it was in the early years of his reign that matters were at their worse, particularly in the West Country where there was open revolt.

Danes Castle and the Siege of Rougemont

Rougemont Castle has been part of Exeter's history for almost a thousand years and parts of this red sandstone bastion still exist, particularly a portion of its great gatehouse which stands only a few yards from the centre of the city.

When Stephen usurped the throne from Matilda one of the barons who strongly supported her was Baldwin de Redvers, a Norman lord whose feudal home was the castle at Plympton. In 1136 he gathered a force and marched on Exeter where he and his men occupied the royal castle of Rougemont in defiance of the king. It was not long before this illegal act brought a response from Stephen who quickly gathered an army and marched on Exeter, laying the castle under siege on arrival. Militarily, however, there was one small problem. He had no garrison for his troops which is where Danes Castle enters the picture... or rather New Castle.

With Rougemont occupied by the rebels the King set about constructing a secure base for his army to fall back to if Baldwin was to mount a counter-attack. It was a simple affair comprising a large earthen mound upon which a wooden stockade would have been built and protected by a moat. Recent site investigations by archaeologists suggest that the castle was in fact never finished. Although the foundations for a timber gatehouse had been dug they had never been utilised, probably because the siege of Rougemont was to end before the building work could be completed.

In fact the siege of Rougemont Castle was to last three months and only ended when the well supplying water to Baldwin and his men ran dry. When he surrendered it brought an end to resistance against the King, at least in Devon.

So what's in a name? Was it New Castle or Danes Castle? Well both are correct in a way. Certainly in mediaeval times it was known as the former and probably so called to distinguish it from the Exeter's great castle of Rougemont. By 1700 however it was referred to as Dane's Castle although there seems to be no apparent explanation for the change of name. Then in 1853 the castle disappeared altogether !

Exeter was growing fast as a city and with it came an increased demand for water. A new reservoir was built and Danes Castle disappeared under the water and became forgotten. In fact it lay forgotten for 140 years until, in 1993, South West Water had to carry out extensive work on the reservoir and on draining it the old castle resurfaced. Realising the importance of the site, South West Water, in consultation with local archaeological groups, reviewed their plans for a new reservoir so that the earthwork could remain uncovered.

It can be viewed at any time and stands in a small grassy park adjacent to Howell Road and the rear wall of Exeter's County Prison. Open entry is at the junction with aptly named Castle Close. Most of the nearby on-street parking is for residents with a few bays for general use.

The above illustration shows how the castle possibly looked in 1136

A section of Danes Castle as it appears today

Part of the ruined gatehouse of Rougemont Castle
as viewed from Castle Street

Plympton Castle

Rougemont Castle was not the only fortress to see action at this time for so, too, did the castle at Plympton. This was the home of Baldwin de Redvers and was of motte and bailey construction crowned by stout walls.

Its downfall came in 1136 when Baldwin left to lay siege to Rougemont castle at Exeter during the revolt against King Stephen. As retribution it is reported that the King sent a force of two hundred knights and archers to take Plympton castle during Baldwin's absence. It fell to the King's forces after a siege following which its defenses were dismantled although it was to achieve some minor prominence some five centuries later when it featured in the Civil War.

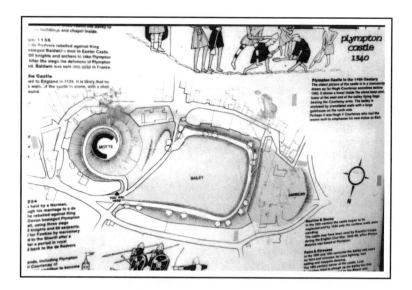

Some of the detail on the Information Board at Plympton Castle

The castle is situated in the centre of Plympton St Maurice, the old part of the town, and routes to it are well signed. Its ruined tower still stands today on top of the motte whereas what was once the bailey below is now a grassy park. It is cared for by the local council and can be seen at any time.

The ruined tower and walls of Plympton Castle are seen here
on top of the grassy motte

23

The Turbulent Middle Ages

Stephen's turbulent reign came to an end in 1154 when he eventually died of illness at the age of fifty. His death also brought to an end the *House of Normandy* dynasty and saw the rise of the *Plantagenets* with the succession of Henry of Anjou as King Henry II. The reigns of the Plantagenets did not bring peace however and the next three hundred years of England's history were not without bloodshed in one place or another. This was the period of the Crusades, the barons' revolt against King John and the signing of the Magna Carta in 1215.

In the mid-thirteenth century there was a further barons' revolt, this time led by Simon de Montfort, whilst 1338 saw the start of the *Hundred Years' War* with France. However, there was also a new threat looming, rivalry for the English throne.

As the fourteenth century drew to an end England was ruled by Richard II. Then, in the century's final year, he was deposed by Henry IV who became the first ruler from the *House of Lancaster*. The new dynasty provided two more kings, Henry V and Henry VI but the latter was facing increasing trouble from the rival *House of York*. It was a rivalry which was to split the country and lead to a succession of wars between the two Houses. These were to last for over thirty years, from around 1455 to 1487, and became known as *'The Wars of the Roses'*.

The Wars of the Roses

When Henry VI was finally deposed in 1461 the *House of York* gained the upper hand and their King, Edward IV, took the throne. He in turn was succeeded by Edward IV and Richard III, all of the *House of York*. One might be forgiven for thinking that a civil war involving two *'royal houses'* so far from Devon would leave the County unscathed but this was not so. For this was a time when barons and earls also pledged their allegiance to one side or the other with the hope that their reward would come when *'their side'* won. It also provided an opportunity to settle one or two local scores.

In Devon two such prominent families were the Courtenays, whose lineage provided the Earls of Devon, and the Bonvilles. The family home of the former was Powderham Castle on the west bank of the Exe and it was a family which supported the Lancastrian cause. Lord Bonville on the other hand was staunchly Yorkist and had lands in the east of the county, at Shute near Axminster. In fact it is reputed that his home was the Headquarters for the Yorkist cause in the Southwest. With both families having their own standing armies, albeit probably small ones, the ingredients for conflict were complete.

Shute Manor, which dates from 1380 and once the Headquarters
for the Yorkist cause in the South West, as it is today

The Battles at Clyst St. Mary

Indeed East Devon was drawn into *'The War of the Roses'* although unfortunately evidence
is rather scant. What we do know, however, is that during the early days of the conflict,
in 1455, there was fierce fighting on two fronts, *'Clisbrigge'* and *'Clist Heath'*. Apart
from the fact that Devon County Council records show these as a *'battle'* little else is
known as to which side was victorious.

However, the site of these battles is easy to view. *'Clisbrigge'* is in fact Clyst Bridge at Clyst
St Mary and is of interest in its own right.

Now closed to vehicular traffic, it is Devon's oldest river crossing with records of its
existence going back as far as 1238. Now scheduled as an Ancient Monument, the
bridge is easily accessible to walkers and is also visible to motorists using the Exeter to
Sidmouth Road. They will catch a glimpse from the left hand side of the dual carriageway
as they approach the Clyst St. Mary roundabout. (Map ref: 192/971910). The Heath,
the other scene of battle, has since disappeared under sand quarries, the motorway and
the development of industrial and business parks. Interestingly, this is not the last we
shall hear of Clyst St Mary.

'Clisbrigge' as it appears today

As to what eventually happened to the two prominent Devon families who featured in the local battles, well it was very much a case of mixed fortunes. The Courtenays continued to prosper and indeed the current Earl of Devon still lives at Powderham Castle. The Bonvilles were not so fortunate. Some five years after the clash at Clyst St.Mary, in February 1461, Lord Bonville was to fall fatally wounded at the Second Battle of St. Albans. However, that was not the only tragedy for the family. Only six weeks earlier, on New Year's Eve, 1460, both his male heirs had been killed at the Battle of Wakefield. The family home at Shute was later to pass into new ownership.

Top body armour of the 15th century

Officially the 'Wars' ended in 1487 with victory for the *House of Lancaster*. However, two years earlier Henry Tudor had gained the throne as Henry VII but later, in a statesmanlike move, he took as his bride Elizabeth, daughter of the late Edward III of the House of York. It was an action which in no small way went to ensure there was future peace between the two Houses.

Chapter Three

THE 16th CENTURY

Henry VIII and the Dissolution of the Monasteries

The 16th century was perhaps one of the most interesting periods of our history when two of our best known monarchs were on the throne, Henry the Eighth and Elizabeth the First. However, in the short eleven-year interval between their reigns England was to have three other monarchs.

The reign of Henry VIII was relatively peaceful and his nickname of the 'Merry Monarch' perhaps provided an indication of his attitude to life. Although he had a serious side, and in particular was responsible for the build up of the country's maritime defences, he is perhaps best remembered for his six wives, problems with the Pope over divorce and his eventual break from Church of Rome which led to the formation of the Church of England. It was these latter events which, whilst not strictly leading to 'battlefields' did nevertheless lead to hostility and 'mayhem' in some quarters. This was highlighted following Henry's edict for the 'Dissolution of the Monasteries' when amongst those to be affected were the great abbeys of Tavistock and Torre.

Tavistock Abbey

The abbey at Tavistock had enjoyed a long and distinguished history having been originally founded by the Saxons and endowed by Ordgar whose daughter was married to the Saxon king, Edgar, a nephew of Athelstan. It was no stranger to strife and had been destroyed before, during a Danish raid on the town. It was subsequently rebuilt by Ordgar's son, Ordulph, only to be sacked again!

It was not until after the Norman conquest that a more substantial building appeared on the site and was to remain, and prosper, until March 1539. That was the date it surrendered to the Commissioners and was then given to John Russell, the first Earl of Bedford, who was responsible for demolishing the abbey church. Other buildings were stripped and left to decay so that much has disappeared with the town's development over the years, particularly in the area around Bedford Square. This does not mean, however, that some parts do not remain for those prepared to search them out.

These include the impressive abbey court gate, one of the busiest of the four great gates giving access to the abbey grounds, which can be seen in Bedford Square. Then, next to the Bedford Hotel, are the remains of Betsy Grimbal's tower, a mediaeval arch once part of the abbey but which today also plays a part in local folklore. One version is that Betsy was a nun who was loved by one of the abbey's monks who then murdered her when the relationship cooled. However a more scholarly view is that it is a corruption of 'The Blessed Grimwald', a 9th century saint.

Torre Abbey

Situated just behind Torquay's long Promenade one can still find plenty of reminders of the once impressive Torre Abbey which, like the others, was largely destroyed during the 'Dissolution'.

Torre Abbey's surviving Gatehouse

Interestingly, however, Torquay owes its popularity as a resort to the conflict of war although it has to be said not in this country. In the late 18th and early 19th centuries the playground of the rich was the South of France and the splendours of Italy. When the Napoleonic Wars raged across Europe and travel to reach such popular places became virtually impossible the rich soon found that the mild climate of the South West around Torbay made an agreeable substitute. What we refer to today as the 'English Riviera' was, two centuries ago, known by the nickname of the 'English Bay of Naples'!

Like Tavistock, however, Torre Abbey was no stranger to conflict. Indeed its construction bears this out for it was uniquely built right on the coast whereas most abbeys were built some distance inland which would afford some measure of protection, firstly against the Danes and later marauding pirates or other such raiders.

It was because of this vulnerable position that Torre Abbey was heavily fortified, in fact in some ways more in keeping with a castle than a religious establishment. As well as three large fortified gatehouses it would probably have had a moat although no trace of this remains today. However, one of the gatehouses has survived together with sections of wall, a tower and the abbey's undercrofts with their vaulted roofs.

One of Torre Abbey's surviving towers

Another part of the abbey also survived for, as was often the case, it was later incorporated into a fine house which was later enlarged by the Carey family. Today it is owned by the Local Authority and houses the local art gallery. This, together with the abbey ruins and its grounds, are open to the public except during the winter months.

However, its most prized building is the 'Spanish Barn'. One of the oldest parts of the abbey, having reputedly been originally built to house the monks who built the abbey, it is at least eight centuries old, 124 feet in length and strongly buttressed. Its new roof was fitted an estimated four hundred years ago!

Why the 'Spanish Barn'? Well this was the name it acquired after an incident which occurred during the attempted Spanish invasion of England in July 1588 when its mighty Armada was routed in the Channel by Sir Francis Drake. The details of this event appear in a later Chapter.

St. Nicholas Priory, Exeter

It was not only the great abbeys which were affected by Henry's edict of 'Dissolution' for It also applied to smaller religious houses such as St. Nicholas Priory in Exeter. It is a local story of events which reputedly occurred here which goes to show the depth of public feeling at the time. The Priory was originally built for monks of the Benedictine Order on land granted to them by William the Conqueror, and dates from the end of the 11th Century. It prospered until 1535 when, under 'King's Orders', the demolition team moved in.

It was when workmen began dismantling the gallery over the rood screen, which separated the choir from the nave, that events took a dramatic turn. A local account says that the work was disrupted when an army of women burst through the door apparently armed with a miscellany of weapons, including pikes and shovels. Intent upon saving the chapel, it seems their immediate target was the workman dismantling the gallery for the account continues that, in fleeing the mob, he sought refuge in the tower. Unfortunately, with the mob in pursuit, and reaching the top, he found only one avenue of escape. He jumped! He lived but not without breaking a number of bones.

The women were subdued soon afterwards and placed in the local prison. However, there was a somewhat happy ending as it was said the Church Commissioners, having eaten a hearty meal, relented and, showing leniency, allowed the women to be released! The Priory was not so lucky and the dismantling of the building and contents continued although some parts were allowed to remain. These can be found in a narrow pedestrian alley known as 'The Mint' which leads off the higher end of Exeter's Fore Street.

The building, which is now in the care of the City Council, is open to visitors on an occasional basis. Viewing much of the exterior is possible at any time but those wishing to enter are advised to check at the Civic Centre Tourist Information Centre for opening times as the Priory tends to be closed during winter months before opening on various days at other times.

St. Nicholas Priory today

However, events such as those demonstrated by the women at the Priory pale into insignificance when viewed in the context of those which occurred following Henry VIII's death in 1547. Succeeded by his sickly ten-year-old son, Edward VI who died when he was only sixteen years of age, the reigns of power were held by two pairs of hands. Matters of State were handled by the Lord Protector Somerset whilst those of the Church were under the supreme power of the staunchly Protestant Archbishop Cranmer. It was the latter's adherence to furthering the Protestant cause, started by Henry VIII, which was to lead to one of the bloodiest events in West County history. Becoming known as the *'Prayer Book Rebellion'*, much of its bloodshed was to occur within East Devon.

The Prayer Book Rebellion

Following the death of Henry VIII, and the accession of the sickly ten-year-old Edward VI, Archbishop Cranmer continued his reforms of the church in England. Within two years he attempted to remove the last vestiges of the Church of Rome by banning the Latin Mass and introducing a new English Book of Common Prayer. It was a move which was to prove decidedly unpopular in many parts of the country but none more so than in Devon and Cornwall in particular.

Few of the peasant stock were literate so the publishing of the new prayer book itself was probably immaterial. To them what mattered was the fact that the Latin Mass they had learnt by rote, and recited by heart through the generations, was to be replaced with a service which was alien to them. The new prayer book was merely a spark.

If Archbishop Cranmer had sewn the seeds for revolt it was in the small Devon village of Sampford Courtenay that violence first erupted although there were also demonstrations of protest in other places too. However, it is at Sampford Courtenay that we start looking at a chain of events which so rapidly escalated and why the date of Whit Sunday, the 9th of June, 1549, will be forever etched in the minds of locals.

That was the day decreed for the English Book of Common Prayer to be first brought into service and on that fateful morning the local vicar introduced the new English Order. However, there were many in the congregation who felt strongly against what they saw as an attack on their faith and promptly tried to force a return to the Latin Mass. It was a recipe for disaster as the protesters fought with those who sympathised with the vicar. Considerable damage was caused inside the church before the violence spread outside into the centre of the village and the square in front of the Church House.

The Church House as it appeared in 1549

The Church House today

As the fighting continued a Justice of the Peace was called to restore order. He was a William Hellyans who, from contemporary reports, took a position on the steps of the Church House from where he apparently used abusive language and, incensing the throng, made matters worse rather than better. How much worse can be gauged by what happened next when some of the crowd, surging forward, hauled him from the steps and hacked him to death. It was an action which was to have dire consequences for thousands.

News of the murder quickly spread and, not only from Sampford Courtenay but also neighbouring parishes, incensed Devonians decided to make their protests known to the highest authority. Neither were they alone for further west in Cornwall similar demonstrations were taking place. Church congregations in towns such as Launceston and Bodmin were of like mind and they, too, decided to march on London.

Meanwhile at Crediton on that Sunday morning, 9th June, local churchgoers also rose in a spontaneous response to the new prayer book and it was not long before they were greeting, in common purpose, the throng from Sampford Courtenay who set up camp on the outskirts of the town. Here their numbers were quickly swollen by the protesters who had marched from Cornwall.

However, the authorities were not oblivious to events and a small force of militia were sent out from Exeter under the leadership of two local knights, Peter and Sir Gawen Carew, both of whom had knowledge of the area. Furthermore, they had a royal warrant effectively authorising them to dispel the protesters, peacefully if possible but otherwise by force. The locals were not to be taken unawares however as their intelligence network quickly enabled them to take defensive action.

Soon the road into Crediton was blocked with barricades and also by men occupying a number of barns from which they put up a spirited resistance. They were proving more than a match for the local militia and might have won the day except for the fact that one of the soldiers, realising the barns had thatched roofs, sent a lighted arrow into the thatch of one of them. As the blaze took hold the defenders had no alternative but to make a hasty retreat but it was an encounter which was to go down in local history and become referred to as either the 'Battle of the Barns' or the 'Burning of the Barns'.

The Carews marched into Crediton confident of routing the rebels and putting an end to the uprising . However, as they entered the town all they encountered was an eerie silence with no sign of the protesters. A feeling of unease fell over them and Sir Peter feared they were being lured into an ambush. Showing discretion rather than valour he quickly withdrew his men and returned to Exeter where he reported that the riot was over.

In fact nothing was further from the truth. More and more protesters were gathering and their leaders reviewed their strategy. They would march on Exeter, the nearest Bishopric. Soon the city was under siege as all the main gates into it became blocked by the rebels. It was not only the men from West Devon, Crediton and Cornwall who were involved for simultaneously another dramatic event was taking place in East Devon.

Being Whit Sunday, it was also a holiday and that morning Walter Raleigh, the father of the more famous Sir Walter, chose to ride from his home at Hayes Barton, East Budleigh, into Exeter to meet with friends. He was a staunch Protestant and also a supporter of the new English Book of Prayer so did not take kindly to the actions of an old crone whom he encountered whilst riding through Clyst St. Mary. She was shuffling her way to church reciting a prayer in Latin as her wizened hands fingered the beads of her rosary. Raleigh apparently stopped and in admonishing her advised in no uncertain terms that she should give up such ancient superstitious ways and obey the new law.

Rather than take heed of this advice however the old woman rushed to the church where it is said they were still using the unauthorised service and she quickly related what had happened. In fact her actions were recorded in the language of the day as **"being impacyente and in agonye - begynneth to upbraye in open churche"**. The account goes on to say that **"shee was beleeved"** whereupon all the men hastened from the church **"lyke a sorte of waspes !"**

The congregation were incensed and, virtually to a man, took off after Walter Raleigh who, from the following eye-witness account, seems lucky to have escaped with his life.

> *"The rebels overtook Walter Raleigh at St. Mary Clyst and were in such choler, and so fell in rages with him, that if he had not shifted himself into the chapel there, and had been rescued by certain mariners of Exmouth which came with him, he had been in great danger of his life, and like to have been murdered."*

Clyst St. Mary Church where the men hastened *'lyke a sorte of waspes'*

Eventually reaching safety beyond the Clyst Bridge, Walter Raleigh continued his way into Exeter where he quickly alerted the authorities to what had happened. Meanwhile in the village the men, realising what they had done, quickly camped on Clyst Heath and threw up a hasty barricade on the ancient Clyst Bridge to protect the village from any reprisals. It was an action which theoretically cut the route from Exeter into East Devon.

As events escalated and the grip on Exeter tightened, the men of East Devon moved on the city to play their part in the siege, holding the South and East Gates. Within a few days what had started as a protest had become a full scale uprising which was to keep Exeter in a stranglehold for a further five weeks. As to numbers taking part, the "King's England" estimates this as *'ten thousand'* and *"The Prayer Book Rebellion'* had become a force to be reckoned with.

Understandably, there was much apprehension in the city, not least amongst the authorities whose first recourse was to look to Lord Russell, the Commander of the local county garrison, for help. However, his troops, small in number, were completely inadequate to deal with the full might of the rebellion so he had no option but to summon reinforcements from the young King and the Governing Council under the Lord Protector Somerset.

It was a plea which was quickly answered and a substantial army was ordered to set out under the command of Lord Grey. It was to be no ordinary army but a hardened force amongst whom were contingents of mercenaries recruited from Germany and Italy. Eventually, after their long march, they met up with Lord Russell's local force at Fenny Meadow (known as Fenny Bridges today), near Honiton, and made camp.

The view of the River Otter from Fenny Bridge today

It was now well into July and conditions in Exeter were bad with the rebels still keeping a strong grip on the city. By sheer weight of numbers their leaders were convinced they were more than a match for any troops the King may send to dislodge them. Full of confidence they decided to take the fight to the army whilst its troops were still camped at Fenny Meadow but, unfortunately for them, they were not military tacticians.

In fact it was a grave tactical error for, although superior in number, the lightly armed rebels were no match for the trained soldiers they were to encounter. Little quarter was given in the fierce battle which ensued and before the end of July it was estimated that over three thousand rebels had been slain in the meadows alongside the banks of the River Otter. It is said the waters of the river ran red with blood in what has been described by some as the *"bloodiest battle ever to take place on English soil."* The site of this bloody carnage is still marked on ordnance survey maps with the crossed swords symbol and the date 1549. It will be found at O.S. Map 192/114989.

Unfortunately, little tangible of the site remains. Known as the Battle of Fenny Meadow, of the meadow little, if any, remains. Firstly, the battle ground was traversed by the railway built in the Victorian era and then further disturbed when the new A30 dual carriageway was opened in 1999. There is still a bridge at Fenny Bridges which, although still narrow, has been renovated and strengthened over the years. However, since the new A30 opened to take most of the traffic away it is much easier to stand and gaze over the parapet at the River Otter still flowing below and towards the railway and the meadows where this bloody event took place over four hundred and fifty years ago.

With their resounding success over the rebels at Fenny Meadow, Lord Russell left his headquarters at Honiton and prepared to march his army on Exeter, finally to relieve the city. Their route took them across what was then mainly heath to make a further camp at Windmill Hill, a rounded hill which offered a good vantage point and was also within easy reach of the city. It can still be recognised today and lies to the south of the A3052, Exeter to Sidmouth road at O.S. Map 192/015901,

By now it was the 2nd of August 1549 and the men of Clyst St. Mary laid plans to attack the army before it moved any further forward. The following day, Saturday 3rd August, they launched their attack but, like their fellow rebels had found earlier at Fenny Bridges, they met a superior armed and disciplined force. They were no match for the troops and, suffering heavy casualties, retreated back to the village. They knew that retribution would follow so existing barricades were strengthened as they prepared to defend the village.

They did not have long to wait. At nine o'clock the next morning, a Sunday, Lord Russell's troops attacked but met fierce resistance. So much so that he made a temporary withdrawal to Windmill Hill whilst he devised new tactics. Then he attacked again, this time with a three-pronged assault with no mercy to be shown. Lord Grey and his mercenaries also met stiff resistance as they tried to take the bridge which was being stoutly defended to prevent his troops reaching Clyst Heath. In fact in the end the troops crossed by means of a ford further upstream and took the bridge by attacking from the rear!

As houses were taken one by one so Russell's troops set them alight and in the end Clyst St. Mary was a village ablaze. There had also been a terrible price paid in terms of human loss with hundreds either slain or taken prisoner. But worse was to come. It is said that those taken prisoner were later herded together on nearby Clyst Heath and brutally killed in cold blood, 900 rebels in all.

Today, the Sowton Industrial Estate and motorway occupy part of this infamous site and the village of Clyst St. Mary has been by-passed by the main road from Exeter to Sidmouth. The razing to the ground of the village in 1549 means that there are no houses left which predate that era. One exception is the Church. Today on the village outskirts, it dates from the 13th century although it has seen periods of restoration through the passing years.

Clyst Bridge and the fringe of Clyst Heath

To capture the essence of the rebellion one really has to stand on the old bridge, both long and narrow. Now, completely pedestrianised, one can look safely over its low parapets and gaze across the damp marshland which borders the River Clyst. This area of once open heath has today become subject to flooding. However, with a little imagination you can visualise the barricade on the bridge as the 'rebels' fought to save their village and preserve their faith and the savage revenge inflicted on those who were taken prisoner.

Following the King's victory at Clyst St. Mary the siege of Exeter collapsed. The rebels retreated, the most defiant heading home to Sampford Courtenay whilst being chased by troops through Crediton en route.

The Parish Church at Sampford Courtenay
where the 'Prayer Book Rebellion' of 1549 both started and ended

The final battle of the 'Prayer Book Rebellion' was to take place back where the bloodshed started, at Sampford Courtenay. At the edge of the village the rebels stood firm to face their adversaries. Despite heavy opposition they put up a gallant rearguard action but in the end were no match for the disciplined troops. Slowly they were beaten back to make one last stand, in the meadow by the church. It was Saturday, 17th August 1549.

Defeat was inevitable and with it came no mercy. Reports estimate that by the end of the day a further six hundred rebels lay dead in the shadow of the church tower. Reference to the battle will be found in the church where one can still see an old oak chest said to have been used on that fateful Whit Sunday when the uprising started.

Afterwards came the retributions as hastily convened courts tried the ring leaders for treason. In Cornwall, for instance, the Mayors of those towns whose citizens had marched in protest were publicly hanged. So, too, was the Squire of Clyst St. Mary, Sir William Winsdale, whose body was left hanging in a village lane where all could see him. However, the most infamous incident of all concerned the Reverend Robert Welsh, the vicar of St. Thomas in Exeter.

The Reverend Robert Welsh's parish church still stands in Cowick Street in the St. Thomas area of the city to the west of the River Exe. Four and half centuries ago it lay outside of the city walls and would have been in an area held by the rebels with whom it has been said the Reverend Welsh had a certain sympathy. It was this which was to lead him to face trial too and also be given a death sentence.

In his case the sentence could hardly have been carried out in a more barbaric manner. Contemporary reports state how a scaffold was erected at the top of St. Thomas's Church tower so as to allow a body to hang over the side. Then the Reverend Welsh was dressed in his full ecclesiastical robes to which were attached numerous religious items associated with the Catholic mass. Finally, bound, he was hanged from his own church tower. One report states that the body was also covered in tar and, as if that wasn't bad enough, reputedly his body was left to hang there for a further four years as a salutary reminder to others who may dissent against the new religion.

Finally the *Prayer Book Rebellion*, which had lasted under two months, was over but had been one of the bloodiest the country had ever seen and all for religious freedom.

The Revd. Welsh's Parish Church of St Thomas

Chapter Four

THREATS FROM THE SEA

Coastal Defences

The Devon coastline has seen threats from the sea for over two thousand years. As we have seen from earlier chapters these were by the Vikings and Danes in the early centuries and later there were raids by pirates and other marauders. It was Henry VIII who finally took a hard look at the country's coastal defences and during his reign he erected a string of coastal forts around our coast. Significant in Devon were the castles at Dartmouth, Kingswear and Salcombe and, to a lesser extent, Bayards Cove Fort also at Dartmouth.

The twin castles of Dartmouth and Kingswear were erected so that a chain could be suspended across the River Dart between them, thus preventing an enemy fleet reaching the town of Dartmouth. There is no record of it ever being used in anger. Today a visit to Dartmouth castle is well worth making for it is in the care of English Heritage and has many points of interest, including an interpretation centre and many ancient cannon. Open throughout the year, it also normally hosts a number of special events during the tourist season. By contrast, Kingswear Castle became a private residence over a hundred years ago and there is no public access.

Bayards Cove Fort is also protected by English Heritage. Tiny in comparison with Dartmouth Castle, it was built around 1534 as a small artillery post to defend the harbour entrance. It is close to the town centre and is open at all times without charge.

The castle at Salcombe had a short life and was soon abandoned. Officially recorded today as Fort Charles, it was temporarily rebuilt by the Royalists during the Civil War and will be briefly mentioned again later.

The Spanish Armada

Almost forty years after the Prayer Book Rebellion one of England's greatest sea battles was fought in the English Channel. Many of the sea captains were Devonshire men and as events unfolded it was one, playing a game of bowls on Plymouth Hoe, whose story was to enter folklore. That man was Francis Drake.

It was July, 1588, and Queen Elizabeth the First had already been on the throne for thirty years during which time she had made an enemy of King Philip II of Spain. He, in turn, had gathered an invasion fleet to sail against England. It was a mighty armada of 129 ships, crewed by eight thousand sailors who not only sailed the vessels but handled their combined firepower of some two thousand cannon. In addition they carried an estimated invasion force of some twenty thousand soldiers.

It was July 19th, 1588, when the Armada was first sighted sailing up the Channel past Cornwall's Lizard Point. An eye witness report says that it was *"an awesome sight with mighty galleons stretched in a crescent shape over seven miles apart from point to point."* It is doubtful if what happened next is still taught in history lessons at school but it certainly was to older generations for it was said that when the news of the approaching invasion force reached the fleet at Plymouth, Drake was reputedly engrossed in a game of bowls on Plymouth Hoe. His reply to the message is now part of folklore for it is alleged he remarked that he had time to finish the game and beat the Spaniards too! Prophetic words as it happened for Drake was no stranger when it came to encounters with the odd Spanish galleon or two.

Because of the prominence of Plymouth in the story many think the great sea battle which led to the defeat of the Spaniards was fought off the South Devon coast. In fact it was fought much further East and only one enemy vessel was taken in local waters. This was the 'Nostra Senora del Rosario' which brings us back to the story of the Spanish Barn at Torre Abbey.

The 'Nostra Senora del Rosario' was a fine ship and in fact the flagship of the Andalusian Squadron. Unfortunately, whilst making her way up through the Channel she collided with another Spanish vessel, was damaged and fell behind. There she became easy prey for Sir Francis Drake who, apparently, accepted her surrender without a shot being fired. Now a prize of war, she was escorted into Torbay from where her captain, a Don Pedro de Valdez, was subsequently taken to London whilst the rest of the crew, some 397 in all, were imprisoned in the great barn of the former abbey at Torre. Later the vessel was removed to Dartmouth but as a result of the incarceration of the crew within the barn it became known as the 'Spanish Barn', a name it has kept ever since.

Associated with this period of the barn's history is also an interesting record that a platoon of demi-lancers was sent from St. Marychurch to guard the prisoners. The twist is, however, that this was not to prevent them escaping but rather to protect them from lynching by the locals. Such was the hysteria surrounding the potential Spanish threat at this time that many of the locals literally believed the Spaniards to be 'child-eating monsters'.

The Spanish Barn

The fact that the Armada was soundly defeated is well known and Drake became a national hero. There is still a bowling green on Plymouth Hoe but whether it is the same one is open to doubt. In any event, the soft green turf once trodden upon by Drake would have been replaced many times over during the past four centuries. As for Drake himself, he still looks seawards from the Hoe in the shape of a larger than life bronze statue whilst his home at Buckland Abbey, to the north of the city, is now looked after by the National Trust and is open to the public.

Teignmouth's French Invasions

The town of Teignmouth has suffered at the hands of the French on at least two occasions and in centuries past their relationship was far from cordial. The first recorded incident came in the 14th Century with the start of the 'Hundred Year's War'. Although all the great land battles, such as Crecy and Agincourt, were fought on French soil, this did not prevent their fleet sailing forth on occasion to find English targets. One of those they chose was Teignmouth when in 1340 a raiding force attacked the town and left it badly damaged.

It is said that the town got its revenge a few years later when it sent a contingent to help Edward III's successful siege of Calais. However, the animosity still continued in other quarters. The Teignmouth men were great fishermen and ventured far to reach the well stocked fishing grounds off the east coast of Canada. In fact part of coastal area to the west of the town is known as Labrador to highlight their Canadian connection. Unfortunately, French fishermen also favoured this area and it appears there was frequent conflict between both sides. Whether these old rivalries were still in the minds of the French in the late 17th Century is not known but once again Teignmouth bore the brunt of their attentions.

Historically events had moved rapidly. The Civil War, covered in a later chapter, was over. The rebellion against James II by James, Duke of Monmouth, was over following his defeat at the Battle of Sedgemoor in 1685. Despite this victory, however, James II was subsequently deposed and fled to France whilst William Prince of Orange landed at Brixham in 1688 to claim the British crown. Meanwhile, in France, James II quickly made allies with the French King, Louis XIV, and persuaded him that a war against England could be to his advantage.

In 1690 the French fleet set sail and was soon engaged in battle with vessels of a combined Anglo-Dutch fleet off the South Coast. It was an encounter from which the French emerged victorious. Flushed with this success the French then sailed westwards looking for other likely targets. Whether past rivalries with Teignmouth were in their mind is not known but the fact is that in July 1690 their fleet anchored offshore and observed the town. One salient factor emerged and that was, unlike Darmouth, there was no protective fort. On the 14th July the French sailed a little closer and swiftly put raiding parties ashore. An account of what happened next appeared in a 'broadsheet' of the day under the heading of *"Great Newes from Teignmouth, Torbay and Exon"* and was said to have been written by an eyewitness. It was reproduced in a book written later in the 19th century and is worth repeating here.

"The French fleet, having been on our coast for several days past, sometimes coasting about, other times at anchor in Torbay, has had this good effect, as to put us in a very good posture of defence. On Saturday morning about daybreak, the whole fleet, being with their galleys, about one hundred and twenty sail, weighed anchor and stood in for a small fishery village called Teignmouth. About five o'clock the galleys drew very near the shoar of the said place, their men of war at the same time played their cannon on the shoar for the space of about an hour or an hour and a half, which scared the poor inhabitants from their cottages, they first taking with them what of any value so short a warning and great fright would permit them. The inhabitants being fled, the invaders immediately landed their men in their long boat to the number of one thousand foot, who being no sooner come in shoar but they presently set the houses on fire; which was soon done, there being never a house in the place but was thatched except the parson's which was covered with Cornish slate. They likewise burnt two or three fishermens' boats in the river and the beacon, and plundered some other straggling houses."

The account then continued:

"Upon the news of this villainous and bold invasion, the militia of the county, horse and foot, immediately made a body and marched after the invaders, shewing a great deal of zeal and resolution to serve their Majesties and country upon this extraordinary occasion ... The invaders having intelligence by their scouts of the posture of our forces and that we were moving towards them, they immediately prepared for to return to their ships ...

48

They landed seven or eight small pieces of cannon just by the shoar side to play on our horse in case we came to quick upon them ..."

That was the end of the invasion. By the time the local militia reached Teignmouth it was a smoking ruin and the French fleet was under sail once more. Many an old score had been settled.

TEIGNMOUTH 300
This plaque was unveiled by
Cllr. Mrs. E. S. Russell
Mayor of Teignmouth
on 14th. July 1990
to commemorate the occupation of the town
by the French Fleet in July 1690
and to welcome representatives of the
twin town of Perros Guirec in Brittany

Today the above plaque is all that reminds visitors of the 'French Invasion'. It will be found not too many yards from the shore in aptly named 'French Street'

Chapter Five

THE CIVIL WAR

The reasons for the Civil War are complex and outside of the local nature of this book. However, it is true to say that there was hardly a parish in England which was not affected in some way or another by the Civil War. In the South West, with its predominant rural communities, it was not surprising that many of its inhabitants should side with the King when the forces of Cromwell tried to enforce the will of Parliament. It was a clash of ideals which would eventually lead to a number of battles and skirmishes in Devon and also lengthy sieges at Exeter and Plymouth. In this chapter we look at some of these events.

The cities of Plymouth and Exeter declared for Parliament although the latter, after being captured by Prince Maurice, was to become a royalist stronghold. Elsewhere in the county a number of the larger towns, such as Barnstaple, also declared for Parliament. In tracing events within the County one is faced with the dilemma of whether to record them in chronological sequence or geographically. In the main the latter course has been taken so as to give the reader a better opportunity of visiting more than one site when in a specific area.

In tracing local events mention has been made of a few places which, whilst not actually the site of a battle, or skirmish, played a prominent role in determining the outcome of the war. There is also the question of definition. For example, when does a 'skirmish' become a 'battle'? Most would probably agree that it is a question of numbers and length of engagement but unfortunately in many cases the historic evidence does not make these facts clear. Fortunately, sites of major battles, where historically recorded, are now marked on Ordnance Survey maps with the 'crossed swords' symbol and the date. However, in military terms 'skirmishes' can play equally important roles and within the context of this book will rank on a par with battles. With this in mind we start in the East with Axminster.

Axminster

Already mentioned earlier in connection with Athelstan, Axminster was to see some fighting during the Civil War which was more by way of a skirmish than a battle. Local records indicate that a force of cavaliers took shelter within the church when besieged by roundheads. In the fighting which followed the tower was badly damaged. Most of the damage has since been repaired although it is said that traces can still be seen from the church interior in the upper reaches.

Shute

This hamlet lies just off the main Axminster to Honiton road and predominant is the fine gatehouse of Shute Barton (O.S. Map 192/ 252975). It has already been mentioned in connection with the Wars of the Roses and at the time of the Civil War was the home of the Pole family, staunch supporters of the King. Originally built as a non-fortified manor it stood little chance when attacked by a force of roundheads who promptly set it ablaze. Fortunately for today's visitors, the fine Tudor gatehouse still remains as, too, do some of its battlement turrets.

The Tudor gatehouse at Shute Barton

Other parts of the building were restored later but still provide an interesting reflection of life in a bygone era. It is still occupied but now in the care of the National Trust. Opening hours are limited during which time conducted tours take visitors through most of the house, including the oldest section.

Honiton

During the Civil War both the King and Cromwell were frequent visitors to the area. One manor house which is known to have hosted King Charles during his visits to Exeter still survives at Honiton. This fine early 17th century house is *Marwood House* which is situated at the eastern end of the High Street. Unlike many such manors which are beyond public gaze, this one can be easily seen through wrought iron gates which open directly from the pavement. However, it is in private occupation so the owner's privacy should be respected.

Ottery St. Mary

Although there is a scarcity of information concerning any major conflicts here during the Civil War, this small East Devon town nevertheless deserves a mention for two reasons. Firstly, during the early stages of the war and loyal to the King, it was for a while the royalist headquarters in the South West. Secondly, it was here that the final stages of the war in the West Country were planned, ironically by the parliamentarians.

The venue for this latter event was Chanters House, the name originating from the fact that this was the domain of the Chanter of Precentor, a senior canon responsible for leading the singing in the adjoining church. It was 1645 and parliamentary troops were already stationed in the town. Their commander, General Fairfax, was staying in the house and it was here he was joined by Cromwell. Together, in the Great Parlour, they planned the next stage of their campaign in the West. It is also reported that whilst here Fairfax was presented with a jewel by Parliament as a reward for his services during their decisive victory at the Battle of Naseby on the 14th June.

Glimpses of Chanters House can be seen from the churchyard although the oldest part, seen here, lies out of sight. The convention room where Cromwell and Fairfax met is to the right of the entrance, as viewed, whilst above is the bedroom used by Cromwell. Enlargement of the property during the early Victorian era included additional wings and the top storey seen here. Today it is in private occupation and the owner's privacy should be respected.

Exeter and the Exe Estuary

This is a story of changing fortunes and also the vital role the sea often played in providing supplies to both sides in the Civil War. Firstly, we shall look at Exeter where, despite many of its population having sympathy for the King, the City declared itself for Parliament.

With much of the surrounding countryside declared royalist it was not surprising that Exeter soon found itself under siege. The city walls formed one of the main areas of defence and a formidable section can still be viewed in Exeter's Northernhay Gardens. The siege turned out to be a protracted one with the citizens being virtually starved into submission by troops under the command of Prince Maurice. After it fell to the Prince it quickly became his principal stronghold in the West.

Looking more closely at these events we start in December 1642, a period when Exeter was under the control of Parliament. In Cornwall one of the King's leading commanders, Sir Ralph Hopton, had raised a Cornish Army and, having received intelligence reports that the garrison at Exeter was weak, set out from Cornwall to take it for the King. Part of the plan included capturing a ship on the River Exe and securing Topsham and Powderham. Initially Hopton's men succeeded in two of their aims. They obtained the ship and secured Powderham. Unfortunately, the same night they lost the ship, it is said by 'neglect'!

For the royalists, supplies now began to run short and, with the extremely cold weather also having an adverse effect upon the men, Hopton decided any prolonged siege of the city was impossible. On the 30th December, 1642, he called upon the city's Mayor, a Christopher Clark, to surrender Exeter to the Crown. The request was refused and the following night, New Year's Eve, Hopton's men made a sudden attack on the parliamentary garrison but were beaten back. Shortly afterwards he received news that roundhead reinforcements, led by the Earl of Stamford, were approaching. Faced with this information and the fact that his supplies were now even shorter, Hopton withdrew his forces back to Cornwall.

Fortunes were soon to change, however, and royalist successes in Cornwall and elsewhere in Devon during the first six months of 1643 saw the King's men moving eastwards. Once more Exeter was under siege, this time by royalist troops under the command of Sir John Berkeley. The last parliamentary footholds in Devon were now becoming desperate and a report from archives show that in the July a relief force of six ships and a thousand men, under the command of the Earl of Warwick, sailed up the Exe in an attempt to break the siege of Exeter.

They passed Powderham without incident and moored at Topsham, then a major port, to land men and secure the banks of the river. Berkeley responded by sinking five ships in the river to block a possible retreat that way by the parliamentary force. It was an action during which the Earl of Warwick lost three of his six ships although most of his men were subsequently able to fight their way out overland.

The following month, August 1643, Prince Maurice, the King's nephew, arrived at Exeter with an army into which had been incorporated Hopton's Cornish Infantry. On the 4th September the city surrendered and thereafter became the main royalist city in the South West until almost the war's end. In July 1644 it is said that King Charles entered the city *'in state'*. Interestingly, his daughter, Henrietta, was born there although unfortunately the house of her birth no longer exists, having been demolished during the redevelopment which followed the blitzes of the Second World War.

But royal fortunes were to swing again and, after Parliament's decisive victory at the Battle of Naseby on the 14th June, 1645, Cromwell once more turned his attentions to the royalist strongholds in the West Country. As his army moved westwards so the cities and towns fell one by one. First Bristol and Bath, then Bridgwater, next Exeter. Within the city supplies were already running low as evidenced by the following extract from a contemporary report:

> *"... provision are so scarce, that Mutton is sold at 10d the pound, Butter at 12d, they have no cheese, wood at 7 or 8 shillings a horse load..."*

Parliament, under Fairfax, eventually reoccupied the city when it finally surrendered to him in April 1646. It is perhaps interesting to record that one of Parliament's great generals, General Monk, spent part of his boyhood in the city and, rather ironically, was later to become the power behind the restoration of the Monarchy.

For those with excellent eyesight, or a good pair of binoculars, walk to the North Street end of the Iron Bridge and gaze upwards to view the unusual weather vane depicted here. Perched high on top of a tall pole of more recent origin, and opposite the public house on the corner, it is capped by a dragon. Reputedly the beast is pot marked. The result, it is said, of being used by roundheads as target practice for their muskets !

Finding reminders of the Civil War in modern-day Exeter is comparatively easy. For example, one only has to walk around the large sections of the ancient city wall which still exist. Originally built by the Romans, then strengthened by the Normans, these also played a significant role in the city's defence during its periods of siege.

However, if seeking a little more in the way of atmosphere then a visit to the restaurant on the first floor of the Ship Inn in St. Martin's Lane may provide it for you. Steeped in history, it was also reputedly one of the favourite haunts of Sir Francis Drake and a quotation of his welcomes visitors at the doorway into the inn.

Here one has to imagine, too, the city a hundred years later, in November 1644, when it was held by royalists. A cavalier officer, a Captain Benet, had been charged with finding quarters for his troops and had done so by billeting them at the inn. We know this because, reputedly, a copy of his report survived and is now reproduced within a leaflet for the restaurant. This is not surprising for he is alleged to have written:

"I have quartered my men in the Ship Inn in Martin's Lane,
An excellent place with good wine, victuals and forage, and
an upright man for host."

St. Martin's Lane and the Ship Inn

The final scene for Exeter's surrender was actually set about five miles east of the city, at Poltimore House in the village of the same name. This was once a fine Tudor mansion, dating from the early 16th Century and set within acres of park land. Sadly in recent years it was badly damaged by fire and what the flames did not destroy vandals did. At the turn of the 21st Century only a shell remained but fortunately, after years of dereliction, legal problems over ownership have been sorted out and with help from English Heritage, local authorities and other bodies restoration work is underway. It was here that the *'Treaty of Exeter'* was negotiated between Sir John Berkeley, the city's royalist governor, and General Fairfax for Parliament. By all accounts the negotiations were a protracted affair, lasting almost a week from 3rd - 9th April 1646. In the end, after much prevarication, Berkeley accepted Fairfax's terms and the resultant Treaty effectively ended the Civil War in the West Country.

A glimpse of Poltimore House as it is today

Treaties can be broken and subsequent actions show that, in Exeter's case, certain terms were not kept by Parliament, particularly with regards to safeguarding the cathedral and churches. It seems that it was the Clergy who were to a great extent responsible for the delays in finalising the surrender terms and their intransigence obviously irked the parliamentarians. It is recorded that, after occupying the city, they fired their muskets into the cathedral's altar, smashed stained glass windows and even rifled some of the tombs to obtain lead from the coffins. If you visit St. Nicholas Priory, which was mentioned in Chapter Three, you may be able to see some of the musket damaged stonework which was removed from the cathedral and later kept there as reminders of those less happy days.

Powderham

Today there is no village of Powderham only a handful of attractive thatched cottages standing near to one of the entrances to the estate of the magnificent castle. The original village has gradually disappeared with time although its ancient red sandstone church, now some six centuries old, still stands close to the west bank of the broad River Exe.

But Powderham is really all about its castle, the building of which commenced at the end of the 14th Century, around 1390, and the Courtenay family whose lineage provide the Earls of Devon. Its first occupant was Sir Philip Courtenay from whom the present Earl is descended. Of French ancestry, the Courtenay family has played a dominant role in history for the best part of thousand years and it has been said that they first began to make their mark during the reign of Henry II (1154-1189).

Of the castle itself there has been much added over the years but some of the original walls, battlements and defensive towers still remain. One of the reasons for much of the later work, carried out during the 18th and 19th Centuries, was to repair the extensive damage caused during the Civil War. Fortunately, the castle has interesting archives so much is on record.

Powderham Castle - rear view

At the time of the Civil War the castle was the domain of Sir William Courtenay, a staunch Royalist who was to play a major role in many battles. Ironically, he was not present at the 'Battle of Powderham' having been wounded in both thighs during the earlier 'Battle of Bridgwater'. Another interesting twist is that he was married to Margaret Waller whose father, Sir William Waller, was one of Cromwell's foremost military tacticians. It was a link which may have had some bearing on future events.

During the war's early stages most of the activity around Powderham centred on the River Exe which was a vital supply route for parliament's garrison at Exeter which was under siege by Lord Hopton. Royalist forces under a Colonel Ashburnam occupied the castle with its strategic position overlooking the river. When in the winter of 1642 Hopton withdrew his forces for a successful campaign in Cornwall, the siege was temporarily lifted and Powderham was evacuated at the same time. However, changing fortunes of war saw Exeter surrender to the King in August, 1643, and, apart from Plymouth which stood out for Parliament, there followed a comparative lull in fighting within Devon.

Following the defeat of the King's army at Naseby in June, 1645, Parliament turned its attention to the West Country and eventually Exeter. However, one obstacle in the path of Fairfax was Powderham Castle which, with other strongholds, provided a defensive ring around the city. As such it was one of their primary targets. One of their contemporary reports describes their first attempt at capture which appears to have been a seaborne assault. It seems they were unaware that Powderham had been reinforced by a contingent of Cornish Infantry. It read as follows:

> *"The design against Powderham-house was this, and thus carried*
> *the Lord's Day December 14 nine of the clock at night. Captaine Deane*
> *(the Controller of Ordnance) was commanded over the Exe with*
> *200 foot and dragoons to possess Powderham-Castle but the enemy*
> *had some few hours before got 150 men into it, unto those that were*
> *there before, which our men not discovering before they landed,*
> *would not return without attempting something."*

Forced to retreat, the roundheads crossed the spit of firm ground across the marshes, which then existed, to occupy the church. Barricading themselves inside one of their first actions was to cut loopholes in the door facing the castle in order to provide firing positions for their muskets. Later these were filled but the square outline of each is still clearly visible today, over three hundred and fifty years later.

One of the wooden inserts in Powderham Church door

The occupation of the church by parliamentary troops obviously caused the garrison at the castle some alarm for one of their contemporary reports read:

"...fearing the Castle would be lost, as well as the River blocked up by the fortifying of this Church; sent therefore on the Monday the fifteenth a party of five hundred foot, who joining with two hundred from the Castle, assaulted our men about seven at night , threw in many granadoes (grenades) amongst them and so continued storming till ten, but were beaten off ..."

Those inside the church soon realised that it was not the best place in which to make a prolonged stand so a decision was made to withdraw. To provide cover for this, a force of roundheads under the command of Sir Hardress Waller marched from Crediton to Exminster in an action which enabled them to retreat across the River Exe during the night of December 17th, 1645, and regroup at Nutwell Grange. With danger averted, the royalists withdrew most of their troops back to Exeter, leaving a force of about 120 men behind under the command of a Major Fletcher.

In January 1645, following the storming of Dartmouth on the 18th, Fairfax moved to Totnes from where it is said that Colonel Hammond had gone to attack Powderham Castle. With defences now at a minimum its eventual fall was inevitable. A contemporary record of its surrender reads as follows:

"On the five and twentieth of this month the General marched in the afternoon towards Powderham Castle where Colonel Hammond was with his Regiment, and that day he sent in a summons to the Castle. They consented to it and surrendered up the Castle upon these terms, to march every man to his one home, leaving all their Arms and Ammunition. Provisions they had but small store in the Castle. Now our next design will be for Exeter."

The castle had in fact surrendered to Colonel Hammond before the arrival of General Fairfax and the castle's archives show that the defences had little hope of holding out against a large parliamentary army with shortage of arms and no provisions left. The terms of surrender were, however, unusual. No prisoners were taken and all those who surrendered were allowed freely to return to their homes on giving up their arms. It is thought that such generosity may have been due to the fact that, as stated earlier, Lady Margaret Courtenay's father was one of Cromwell's foremost commanders.

Following the royalist surrender Powderham was occupied by Parliament as an important garrison from which to block the River Exe and prevent supplies reaching the besieged city of Exeter. When it no longer served their purpose much of it was rendered unfit for any further military use and remained in a largely ruined state until restored during the 18th and 19th Centuries.

We cannot leave the history of Powderham and its role in the Civil War without one mystery. Where was Powderham Fort? Again we turn to contemporary records which show that even though the castle had fallen there was still an element of royalist resistance in the area. An account written after the castle's surrender records the following:

"Colonel Hammond intends against Powderham Fort, a stronghold of the enemies upon the River near Exeter, in which are several pieces of Ordinance (for there were none in the Castle), 150 men whereof 50 got out of Exeter on Saturday night ..."

It appears the fort held out until April, 1646, when Exeter finally surrendered to Fairfax but where it stood is a mystery. Powderham's archives have a record of its existence but none of its location. Similarly, a search of the county records drew a blank for there appears to be no contemporary map of the area with it shown either. The Castle's Archivist suggests that, strategically, the best position for such a fort would be where the river narrows, probably close to where the Turf Hotel now stands ... but that is only a guess!

Today Powderham, with its river frontage and acres of deer park, is one of Devon's foremost tourist attractions. It is located on the main Exeter to Dawlish road (O.S.Map 192/968836), with one of its main entrances in the village of Kenton. For up to date information and opening times contact any local Tourist Information Centre or the Powderham Estate Office.

If visiting the church for its Civil War connections you will find in the churchyard a victim of a much later war. Near the seaward side is a lone grave of white Portland stone easily distinguishable from its more sombre neighbours. Under the insignia of the Royal Air Force it simply reads "Sergeant Pilot M.S. Gilbert RAF. Killed 30th October 1942. Aged 19 years." He was the son of the then Agent for the Powderham Estate.

Exmouth

The strategic importance of the River Exe as a supply route to both sides during the Civil War has already been well covered although little has been said about Exmouth and its commanding position at the river mouth. The town we know today did not exist until bathing places became fashionable in the 18th Century, before which there were a few fishing cottages and the villages of Littleham and Withycombe.

Whilst there is little record of any major fighting in the area, a 'blue plaque' records the fact that a battery of cannon was installed on the 'Gun Cliff', an area now a public park known as Gunfield Gardens and situated on the sea front close to the Pavilion.

Exmouth's Gunfield Gardens

From the coast we now examine how the Civil War affected areas to the North of Exeter, starting with Crediton.

Crediton

About nine miles north of Exeter, Crediton is better known for being the birthplace of St. Boniface In 680 AD rather than any great participation in the Civil War. Nevertheless, like most towns in Devon, it was to have its moments and visitors will find these highlights have been briefly outlined on a large chronological table at the rear of its magnificent church. No doubt there were other minor events but it seems that during the first two years of the conflict there was nothing worthy to note.

The table first records that in 1644 Prince Maurice and the royalist army were in the town. Then, in July of that year, the Earl of Essex and his parliamentary army marched through the town. That must have been early in the month and they could not have stayed long for the table then records that, on the 27th July, King Charles held a review of his troops on Lord's Meadow.

Again we have evidence of changing fortunes for the table also records that in October, 1645, Oliver Cromwell joined Sir Thomas Fairfax for a review of their parliamentary army, also on Lord's Meadow! Apparently, they also attended divine worship in the church next day. There is, however, one small hint that there may have been a skirmish

63

between the opposing sides. This is a record, also to be found within the church. It simply reads *"Twelve soldiers are buried this year in Crediton."*

Elsewhere any buildings which may have been associated with the Civil War, other than the church, probably disappeared in the 'Great Fire' of 1743 when 460 houses were destroyed. As the record states, *"The West Town is all burned from Mr Philip Dicker's to Mr Butler's and back again to the cross."* Such was the ferociousness of the fire that John Wesley, the founder of Methodism, on seeing the charred ruins was said to ask, *"Are the people of this place warned to seek God ?"*

Despite this catastrophe Crediton is still worth a visit even though the site of the army reviews, Lord's Meadow, is now the town's industrial estate. It is the fine church, built on Norman foundations, which makes any visit worthwhile. For those interested in the Civil War in particular, ask if it's possible to see the Governors' Room which is clearly visible in the photograph below.

Approached by a winding staircase this is where the twelve Governors met to control the church which had been bought by the townspeople from Henry VIII when the collegiate church was dissolved in 1547.

Little has changed in the room since those days except that it now houses a number of historic artifacts, including mementos of the Civil War.

About six miles to the north east of Crediton lies Cadbury Camp, once a base for Cromwell's forces.

Cadbury Camp

The strategic position of this former iron-age fort, (O.S. Map 192/913053), was not lost on either Cromwell or General Fairfax. Occupying a commanding hilltop position its existing earthwork embankments provided Parliament's army with ready-made defences. Furthermore, it offered an excellent base from which to launch assaults on two nearby royalist strongholds, Bickleigh castle a mere couple of miles away and the castle at Tiverton about five miles further.

Today the site remains accessible by the public via a marked footpath from the minor road between Thorverton and Cadbury. Parking is provided in a small lay-by nearby although it is rather limited. The approach from the road is by an uneven track in the early stages followed by a footpath skirting a large field. Good walking shoes or boots are advisable and allow at least half an hour for the walk there and back. The views from the top are well worth the effort.

At the foot of the hill, close to the start of the track, is Cadbury House. It dates from the early part of the 16th Century although it has changed over the years. It is understood that whilst most of the troops were camped on the hill itself, many of the officers billeted themselves in the surrounding houses for a higher degree of comfort. Although no record exists in respect of Cadbury House there is little doubt that it was one of those chosen. Today it is in private occupation and generally hidden from view behind a high wall. The owner's privacy should be respected.

There is also an interesting tale told about this location. On some nights, it is said, the susceptible can still hear the sound of soldiers' marching feet coming down the track from the camp!

Less than a mile away to the south, on the minor road to Bowley, is a delightful thatched cottage by the roadside which goes under the name of 'Parliament Cottage'. Four centuries ago the main road to Exeter used to run close to here and research by the owner confirms that during the Civil War parliament's troops were billeted in the cottage. In addition, whilst apparently there is no documentary evidence, there is a strong local tradition that Cromwell held an emergency meeting of Parliament within the living room whilst engaged in his military operations. As its owner says, **"It's been known as Parliament Cottage for centuries so how else would it have got its name?"**

Like Cadbury House, the cottage is also a private dwelling although being located by the roadside it is easy to see the stout, buttressed cob walls beneath the sloping thatched roof. Other than perhaps by glimpsing whilst passing, once again the owner's privacy should be respected.

Bickleigh

Situated on the banks of the upper Exe, the view from Bickleigh's narrow bridge towards a scenic waterside cottage has been photographed and literally reproduced a thousand times. However, this is not our primary objective but rather Bickleigh Castle which is situated along a minor road on the west bank of the river, (O.S. Map 192/935068).

65

There have been dwellings on this site since Saxon times with an entry in the Domesday Book showing the then occupant to be Alward, a Saxon. Then, about nine hundred years ago, the land passed into the hands of a Norman family, the *de Bickleighs* from whom the estate, and later the nearby village, achieved its name. Other Norman owners followed as did the transition from Saxon dwelling to Norman Castle and around 1410 it became one of the estates owned by the powerful Courtenays who already owned the castles at Powderham and Tiverton, Bickleigh being purchased as a portion of the younger sons. Later, by way of a marriage dowry, it passed to the Carew family who remained its owners until the early 20th Century.

The castle was to last function as such during the Civil War when its owner was Sir Henry Carew. He was a supporter of the royalist cause and, not surprisingly, the castle's death knell was sounded when Parliament's most successful general, Sir Thomas Fairfax, made camp with a substantial army at nearby Cadbury Camp. Despite its name, Bickleigh Castle had been built more for the comforts of a well-fortified manor than a substantial castle and was unable to sustain a prolonged onslaught. It soon fell to Fairfax who at once ordered the fortified wings to the north and west of the inner courtyard to be destroyed. No longer capable of any military use, Sir Henry was allowed to remain there until he died in 1681. Sadly, he left no male heirs and over a period of time the buildings gradually fell into disrepair.

Restoration work on the castle commenced early in the 20th Century and eventually, in 1970, passed into the hands of the Boxall family who trace their roots back to the Dukes of Northumberland. Today it looks quite impressive with its red sandstone exterior.

The Great Hall still remains, so too does the Gatehouse which is used to house a collection of Cromwellian arms and armour. Outside part of the moat can still be seen albeit now incorporated into a water garden. Situated in an enclosure across the road is the castle's detached 11th Century Norman chapel which is said to be the oldest complete building in the county.

Evidence of Civil War 'bullet holes' comes in an unexpected quarter. If you decide to make a tour of the castle's interior look for a 17th Century portrait of an Abbess which now hangs in the former guardroom. It is a known fact that many of the roundhead soldiers had little respect for religious icons and any reminders of the Catholic faith. To them the portrait was just one more example and they wasted no time in firing a musket shot or two at it. Although it has since been restored the five round holes left by the shot have been carefully preserved and are clearly visible as a reminder of the turbulent and often violent period.

Bickleigh Castle as it appears today

The castle is open to the public during afternoons but the days vary according to season. For up to date information the castle can be phoned during normal business hours or alternatively leaflets are available at most local Information Centres.

Tiverton

Originally known as Twyford in Saxon days, Tiverton has a very long history and was probably at its economic ascendancy during the 16th - 17th Centuries when fortunes were made through the woollen industry. Later, in the 19th Century came the manufacture of lace and the rise of the Heathcoat dynasty. Many examples of the town's early heritage were lost when a number of fires swept the town during the 18th Century although a few still remain. Arguably the most impressive of these is the town's castle.

Situated close to the town centre, Tiverton Castle stands next to the parish church of St. Peter, the tower of which makes a good landmark, although in chronological terms the castle predates its neighbour by some centuries. In fact its origins date from soon after the Norman conquest when it was a formidable fortress overlooking the River Exe. It was the original home of the Courtenay family who provide the Earls of Devon and have already been mentioned a number of times. It remained their home until they moved out to establish the family seat at Powderham Castle. Through the passage of time some of the castle's original glory may have been lost but fortunately enough remains to give a glimpse of its historic and sometimes turbulent past when the Civil War finally ended its life as a fortress.

Once again the name of Fairfax comes up and the story of Tiverton is synonymous with that of Cadbury and Bickleigh which we have already covered. It was October, 1645, when Fairfax marched on Tiverton with his parliamentary army. What happened next is related in graphic but simple terms within a report to Parliament which was written at nine o'clock on the night of the 19th of the month. It reads:

"On Friday, the 17th instant, our General Sir Thomas Fairfax sat down before Tiverton Castle and Church, to take them in and summoned the enemy to deliver them up, of which being denied, we planted our batteries against them, which went forwards that day and next. On Saturday October 18 instant, our batteries were finished by the afternoon and on this day being the Lord's Day October 19 instant, the General caused several great pieces to be placed on the batteries against the Castles so that they were ready to play by break of day, and all our cannon began to play about seven o'clock in the morning, against the castle, and the Enemy from thence answered us with their pieces but did no execution upon us.

And after many shot that we had made against them, a Cannonier by one shot gallantly performed his business, for he broke the chain of the drawbridge with a bullet, which passeth over to the entrance of the Castle, which falling down, the chain being broken, our Soldiers fell on without any further order from the General. They being loath to lose such an opportunity, and loving rather to fight than look on when god gives them such occasion, which took good effect, for they soon possessed themselves of all, they presently entered the Castle and Church, in which we had four men slain: yet such is the mild and gentle carriage of the General, and his desire to spare the effusion of blood, as much as may be, that notwithstanding they took it by storm, yet he himself gave the command that quarter should be given to all those who were alive."

The report continues to say that they captured the castle's governor, Sir Gilbert Talbot, twenty other officers and two hundred soldiers. Four cannon were also seized along with a good store of arms and ammunition and an abundance of treasure which it records was divided later amongst the victorious soldiers. Finally it records that the castle was very strong and all works regular. From this account it appears that the royalist defenders at Tiverton fell to the lucky shot from a cannon which shattered the drawbridge chain!

Following the castle's fall it suffered the same as all the others, its fortifications were destroyed so that it would be of no further military use. Fortunately for today's visitors, sufficient remains to make a visit interesting. Amongst the parts still remaining are the impressive main gate which still acts as the castle entrance, a number of the walls and towers. The castle is still occupied and in private ownership but opens to the public at regular intervals, mainly during the afternoons in the tourist season. One of its main exhibits is an impressive armoury which displays a fine collection of Civil War weapons and pieces of armour which occasionally members of the public are invited to try on.

For those who are perhaps interested in reading Parliament's view of the battle, copies of their reports are kept at the Westcountry Studies Centre, Castle Street, Exeter.

Part of the cover of one such report is reproduced below and it was from this that the extracts used in this section were taken.

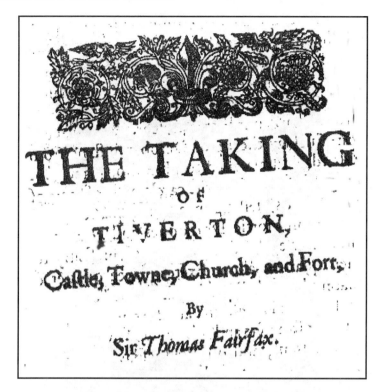

THE TAKING

OF

TIVERTON,

Caſtle, Towne, Church, and Fort,

By

Sir Thomas Fairfax.

(3)

chaine of the Draw-bridge with a bullet, which paſſeth over to the entrance
of the Caſtle, which falling downe, the
chaine being ſo broken, our Souldiers
fell on without any further order from
the Generall, they being loth to loſe
ſuch an opportunitie

Whilst today's visitors to the castle will find little trace of the drawbridge, or the lucky cannon shot which brought about its fall, there is nevertheless other evidence of the battle. For this, look at one of the surviving towers where the damage you see was reputedly caused by cannon shot.

One of Tiverton Castle's surviving towers
It is said that the holes in these are the results of being hit by cannon balls

Tiverton Castle Gatehouse

Details of opening hours are published on the nearby notice and the public entrance is through the arch.

North Devon

Moving northwards from Tiverton we come to North Devon where, fortunately, a few visual reminders of the Civil War still remain. It was also the scene of one of the West's major battles. However, we begin at Barnstaple, the area's largest town, commercial centre and, arguably, England's oldest borough.

Barnstaple

At the outbreak of the Civil War Barnstaple quickly proclaimed its support for Parliament although it was to surrender to the Crown the following year. There is also a record that in July, 1644, there was a skirmish when supporters of Parliament tried to take over the town but were defeated. Very good evidence of this event will be found at the Penrose Almshouse in Litchdon Street, not far from the clock tower.

The almshouses were built in 1627 from an endowment provided by John Penrose who had been Mayor of the Borough. They comprise about twenty dwellings arranged around a pleasant enclosed courtyard, the entrance to which is through an arched gateway flanked on either side by an impressive colonnade. The homes are occupied and a glimpse of the courtyard through the arch is usually sufficient without further disturbing the privacy of the residents. The Trustees' Board Room may be visited, however, with permission of the warden.

Evidence of the Civil War may be seen from the street pavement but it is better to enter the colonnade where, at each end, one will see a heavy oak door blackened with age. Look closely at the one to the left which leads to the Board Room and it will be seen to be riddled with holes. A nearby notice states that these were caused by musket shots fired by roundheads during their campaign to recapture the town.

Within the Board Room are a number of records pertaining to the almshouses and also a couple of cannon balls recovered during more recent renovations. Amongst other exhibits, and hanging on the wall, is another account of how the holes appeared in the door. It is an extract from Barnstaple Records and states:

1644 Mem: *"that the 1st July 1644 a day never to be forgotten by the inhabitants of Barnstaple for God's mercie and faviour, shewed that in miraculous deliverance of them from that bloody conspiracy of some of our neighbours in inviting and bringing in five or six hundred horse and foot, being French, Irish and some English against the town with purpose to have put all therein to the sword and to have possession of the whole town. On the 9th July, one Howard, a Lieutenant who was taken prisoner in the fight was hanged at the High Cross at Barnstaple (see Parish Register)."*

Below is a note attributed to a T. Wainwright who writes in the records:

"The fighting took place on Litchdon Green and there is little doubt that the bullet holes to be seen in the oaken door at Litchdon Almshouses were made in the course of the attack."

The various nationalities involved in the attack were explained by the Curator who said that a number of Irish Protestants supported Cromwell whilst the French were in fact Huguenots who had escaped persecution in France, many of whom had settled in the Barnstaple area.

Bideford

This attractive North Devon town which straddles the River Torridge is perhaps best known for its mediaeval bridge, almost 700 feet in length and comprising twenty-four arches each of a different span. It has an interesting history which encompasses its most famous son, Sir Richard Grenville, a sea captain who fought with Drake against the Spanish, to later connections with the great Victorian novelist Charles Kingsley.

The River Torridge has provided Bideford with a route to the sea for centuries. It is still a working port, albeit a small one, and during the Civil War whoever controlled this waterway had a distinct advantage. This was a factor foreseen by Parliament very early on and they wasted little time in erecting a substantial fort on high ground at 'East the Water'. As the name suggests, this lies east of the Torridge and those wishing to visit it should cross the bridge from the main town and then proceed up the hill on the far side. A turning to the left will lead to very pleasant municipal gardens set on a slope and with the fort located at its highest point. Those making the climb will be rewarded by excellent views of both Bideford and the River Torridge below.

The fort is one of the very few which were specifically built during the Civil War to have survived until today. Constructed by Major General Chudleigh in 1642, it is not known whether it actually saw any action although its cannon point directly towards the town and river. It is now known as 'Chudleigh Fort' after the Parliamentary General who built it.

Chudleigh Fort, Bideford
Civil War cannon still point towards the Torridge and the town

Weare Gifford

Proceeding upstream along the River Torridge from Bideford, the village of Weare Gifford lies on the eastern bank and can be reached by way of a minor road. It supports an ancient church and a fine manor house dating from the 15th century. It was once the home of the Fortescue family and like many mediaeval manors was once fortified for defensive purposes. It was these fortifications which were to lead to problems during the Civil War.

There is a record that parliamentary troops attacked the manor, severely damaging the outer walls in such a way that they could be of no military value. Fortunately, the hall was saved which was a blessing because it is said to contain one of Devon's finest oak carved roofs. The old gatehouse also remained. The manor is in private occupation but glimpses of it can be obtained both in the village and by those who follow the 'Tarka Trail' between Bideford and Torrington.

Torrington

Arguably there is no better place in Devon to get a feel for the Civil War than here in Torrington, or Great Torrington to give it its proper name. Perched high on a hill above the waters of the River Torridge, there is evidence that this strategic position has been occupied ever since early man. Later the Saxons were here and the town had achieved status as a 'fair and market town' before the 13th Century. A feudal castle was built during the 12th Century barons' wars for a record exists that it had been built without the King's permission and the Sheriff of Devon had been ordered to destroy it in 1228. Later another castle was built, this time with permission, but apart from a grassy knoll no trace of this remains either.

During the Civil War the town declared for the King and was garrisoned by royalist troops under the command of a Colonel Digby. In the first skirmish, which occurred during 1643, it is recorded that his men successfully repulsed a roundhead attack. A second attack was not made for almost three years but on that occasion there was a completely different outcome.

It was 1646 and the town's royalist troops, comprising the Prince of Wales's army, were now under the command of the experienced Hopton who had as his commanders Lords Capel and Wentworth. The skills of these men were however matched on the other side by one of Parliament's most able generals, Sir Thomas Fairfax, then 34 years of age. On the night of Monday, February 16th, he marched his troops in from the East, an area of relatively level ground and thus avoided a difficult uphill advance.

In the ensuing battle many of the town's buildings were severely damaged and there was considerable loss of life, but none so tragically lost as those who died in the parish church. It was an incident which was to become deeply etched in the history of Torrington.

As so often happened during the Civil War, church buildings were commandeered for military purposes and Torrington's parish church was no exception. It would appear that Hopton had used it to store his army's gunpowder supplies and a figure of eighty barrels has been mentioned. When the town fell to Fairfax the church became a makeshift prison and some two hundred royalists prisoners were incarcerated there. What happened next is open to speculation but it seems likely that in the church's dark interior one of the prisoners lit a naked flame in the vicinity of the gunpowder store with the result there was an instant and massive explosion. The church was wrecked and all the prisoners were killed.

A contemporary report, dated shortly after the battle and presented to Parliament, gives a most graphic description of the events and is worth quoting here, at least in part.

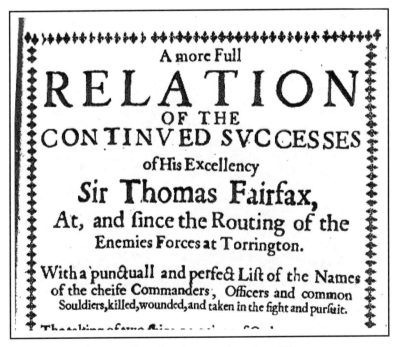

A more Full

RELATION
OF THE
CONTINVED SVCCESSES
of His Excellency

Sir Thomas Fairfax,
At, and fince the Routing of the
Enemies Forces at Torrington.

With a punctuall and perfect Lift of the Names of the cheife Commanders, Officers and common Souldiers, killed, wounded, and taken in the fight and purfuit.

An extract from the above report reads as follows:

" The providence of God in that passage of blowing up of the church is very remarkable, for although the lead, timber and stones of the church were cast several ways for half a miles from the town, yet not any man, woman or child was hurt, besides those blown up in the church which now upon credible information were certified to be near 200 of the enemies which were prisoners there.

Every house in the Town was shaken and shattered with the blow and the falling of lead and timbers. The lead fell thick in the street when the General and Lieutenant General entered and a horse near the General was knocked on the head with a piece of lead, but through God's mercies he nor any of his attendants had any hurt. This was the Lord's doing and it is marvellous in our eyes ..."

The church was rebuilt five years later but some parts of the original still exist, mainly within the southeast chapel. There is however a more poignant reminder of this tragic incident. Enter the church precincts by way of the alley at the junction of High Street and Fore Street and take the path towards the west door. You will see a long mound in the centre of the pathway with a few trees growing from it. Reputedly this is the mass burial grave of those who were killed in the explosion.

During the Battle of Torrington it has been estimated that some 15,000 troops from both sides were engaged and the importance of Parliament's victory on this occasion cannot be underestimated. It is said to have been the battle which determined the end of any major Royalist resistance in the West Country.

A replica of Torrington Church blazes on the 350th anniversary

Today Torrington has turned the Civil War into a tourist attraction with a permanent 'family attraction' entitled 'Torrington 1646." It is open throughout the year, except for a period during the winter, and is located adjacent to Castle Hill car park. Visitors to the exhibition are taken back to the 17th Century through a 'time tunnel' assisted by costumed guides who act as 'first person' interpreters using the dialogue of the period. To celebrate the 350th anniversary of the battle a major pageant was held on the town common which ended with a 'blowing-up' of the church!

Hatherleigh

Traveling South from Torrington on the A386, perhaps to visit Okehampton or Prayer Book Rebellion connections at Sampford Courtenay, your route will take you through the pleasant market town of Hatherleigh. The local town council, with help from local businessmen, have produced an informative leaflet which combines a town trail and street map leading visitors to the local attractions and places of interest. One of these is Hatherleigh Moor, a fifteen minute uphill walk along Victoria Road. It is thought that the moor's 430 acres were given to the town by the Abbot of Tavistock as long ago as the 14th Century.

Three hundred years later, in 1644, it was to be the scene of a Civil War encounter between cavaliers and roundheads. Recorded as a 'skirmish' between opposing horsemen it is said that a force of six hundred roundheads were routed by King's cavaliers under the command of Sir Francis Doddington. It must have been an awesome sight to witness so many horsemen thundering across the open heath in this otherwise peaceful part of Devon.

Okehampton

Visitors to this North Dartmoor market town today are drawn by its closeness to the moor itself and attractions such as the gaunt ruins of its imposing Norman castle or the Museum of Dartmoor Life. Few will give the Civil War a second thought and yet, buried in the churchyard of the parish church, is a young life which to many sums up the futility of war. He was Sidney Godolphin.

Records show he was born in Godolphin, Cornwall, in 1610 and was well educated enough to go to university at Oxford by the age of fourteen. By the age of eighteen he was representing his home constituency as a Member of Parliament, sitting in both the Long and Short Parliaments where it is said he made many friends.

He also became noted as a 'poet of some distinction', although evidence of his work today is rather sparse, and it has been said that his works were mainly of a religious nature or else 'love lyrics'. Some commentators also say that, had he lived, his works would have been highly acclaimed. But this was not to be and his young life was cut short.

When the Civil War started in 1642 it is said that Sidney Godolphin made a solemn speech to his fellow members in Parliament and then withdrew. He then left the nation's capital to return to his native Cornwall in order to raise a body of horsemen to fight for the cause of the King. He did not live long enough to carry out his intention and the story of how he met his death is related under 'Chagford'.

As to actual fighting in or around Okehampton itself there were undoubtedly a few 'skirmishes'. Such evidence comes from a quote in a letter dated *'Jan.10, 1645, 9 in the morning'* and written to The Honorable William Lenthall Esq., Speaker of the Honorable House of Commons. It opens:

" Sir, whilst Sir Hardres Waller yesterday amused the enemy with a party of horse and foot near Okehampton ..."

Reading the letter today one can only surmise whether the royalist enemy were really amused but it is extremely unlikely given the content of a further letter written from Ashburton the following day. This said:

" ... Since the writing hereof, Intelligence has come, Sir Hardres Waller hath beaten up their quarters at Okehampton and taken many prisoners, so they are alarmed on all hands...".

Before leaving the Okehampton area to return towards South Devon those who like to visit actual battle scenes may like to travel a few miles west along the A30 as far as Sourton Cross for it was here one of the first encounters between the royalists and roundheads in Devon was fought.

It was 1643 and Plymouth was firmly under Parliament's control and defended by the Earl of Stamford and his local commander, a Colonel Wardlaw. Opposing him was the royalist commander, Lord Hopton, who lacked the resources to launch a full-scale attack on the city. Across the Tamar, in Cornwall, the few parliamentary resources were under the control of a young Devonian officer, James Chudleigh. He and Hopton were to clash at Sourton Down on 25th April, 1643.

The battle site has been partially bisected by the new A30 dual carriageway at its junction with the A386 to Tavistock. County records show its location at O.S. Map 191/546918 and visitors to the area just north of the main road can still make out a number of low embankments now mainly covered by gorse. The encounter has been given 'battle' status although some historians say it was a 'skirmish'. It appears that Hopton was moving a large number of men and supplies towards North Cornwall and when news of this manoeuvre reached Chudleigh he lay in wait and laid an ambush. The numbers involved are not known but it is recorded that Hopton was defeated, losing a thousand muskets and all his correspondence.

Chagford

Following the Civil War trail from Okehampton we come to Chagford, a small town with a great history for it was once one of the county's powerful stannary towns with a charter dating back to 1305. As a centre for the Dartmoor tin mining industry, it was here the early tinners would bring their metals for assay, be assessed for any tax and then sell their product to the merchants. With the decline of tinning Chagford prospered for a while with the woollen trade and then became a moorland agricultural centre. Although agriculture is still important in recent years it has been overtaken by tourism and whilst in the town many tourists will no doubt quench their thirst, or perhaps have a meal, at the 'Three Crowns'.

This is an attractive thatched inn of 15th Century origins with its mullion windows still overlooking the parish church in the centre of town. Few entering through the ancient porch will be aware of the history made here in February 1643.

The Three Crowns Inn at Chagford

The Civil War was still only months old but already its presence was being felt in the town and roundhead soldiers had occupied the inn. In an effort to oust them a small party of royalists attacked the inn and amongst them was the young Sidney Godolphin, previously mentioned, who was on his way home to raise a Cornish contingent for the King. In the skirmish there was the inevitable exchange of musket fire during which Sidney Godolphin was shot as he tried to fight his way into the premises. It is said that the shot entered him *'a little above the knee'* and he immediately fell on the spot and *'died on the instant.'* Given today's medical knowledge one must wonder how accurate the contemporary report is for it seems unlikely a wound to the lower thigh would prove fatal, at least not 'on the instant.'

About ten miles southeast of Chagford lies another busy moorland fringe town, Bovey Tracy. This, too, has Civil War connections.

Bovey Tracy

Those who study an Ordnance Survey map will see that at O.S. Map 191/821769 there is the crossed swords symbol and the words 'Bovey Heath 1646'. For the visitor the town offers one or two possibilities for those seeking a reminder of the Civil War.

It was New Year, 1646, when the war reached Bovey in earnest. There was already a large royalist brigade in the area and, as was so often the case, the cavalier officers would find good lodgings for themselves. In Bovey one of the houses occupied was 'Front House' which today is a guest house and will be found at the higher end of the main street almost opposite the Town Hall.

Whilst there have been a number of changes made to the building, two vertical pillars of the original stone work are still visible. However, it is not the house which is so important but rather what happened there for it was an incident which is now part of the town's folklore. There are, however, two slightly differing versions. One is referred to in a contemporary letter whilst the other has perhaps been rather embellished with the passage of time.

The popular version is that with seemingly little military activity, the cavalier officers at Front House were enjoying a sociable round of cards with a pile of stake money growing on the table in front of them. War was furthest from their minds when one of them, looking up from his hand of cards, espied a large contingent of roundheads coming towards the house. Parliament had launched a surprise attack and the town was about to be invaded. The cavaliers knew that if caught within the house they had little chance of survival and their escape route was about to be cut off. It was at this point that one of the cavaliers showed a shrewd understanding of human nature.

Parliament's troops were rarely paid and were often left to rely on booty taken in battle and armed with this knowledge it took but a split second for the officer to spring into action. Scooping up all the money on the card table, he flung open the window and threw all the coins into the road in front of the advancing roundheads. The reaction was predictable. The roundheads momentarily paused and then there was a mad scramble as they made a mad dash to retrieve as many coins as possible. For the cavaliers it provided a moment of chance. Grabbing only their swords, they executed a hasty exit and made good their escape to join the main body of their own troops on the outskirts of town.

Whether they were to enjoy the benefits of their escape for long is not known for on the 9th January, 1646, there was a mighty battle fought on Bovey Heath at the outskirts of town during which the royalist brigade, under the command of Lord Wentworth, met a superior parliamentary force led by Cromwell and Fairfax. In the end it was reported that the royalists had been 'disastrously defeated'. A letter sent from Ashburton on the 11th January to the Honoured Edmund Prideaux Esq., a Member of the House of Commons, mentions briefly the outcome of the battle and also makes a passing reference to the incident at Front House although making no reference to the game of cards. It states:

"Sir, I thought fit to send this express unto you , for the better confirmation of that I writ unto you yesterday. We took at Bovy four hundred horse at least and seven horse Colours, whereof one is the King's having the crown and C.R. Upon it. A Major and some officers and soldiers were taken prisoners. We lost but one man. Divers of the enemy were wounded, some slain; some of their chief officers being in a house, shut the door, and threw out at the window about ten pounds in silver, which the foot soldiers were so busy about getting their shares that the officers escaped in the meanwhile over the River through the darkness of the night ..."

The Battle of Bovey Heath has certainly not been forgotten by the town. Although part of the battleground has now disappeared under the Heathfield Industrial Estate a visitor to the area is left in no doubt as to its historical connections as the above road sign shows.

Fortunately, towards the town itself much of the heath still remains to be enjoyed by walkers although watch out for 'off the road' bikers! See if you can find the wooden cross erected in memory of those who fell in battle and look, too, for the redoubts, or defensive ditches, which still survive in the area.

The lonely wooden cross which marks the Battle of Bovey Heath

Before leaving Bovey Tracy there is one more local story to be told and this relates to the parish church where the vicar at the time of the Civil War was the Reverend James Forbes. A royalist, he had at one time been chaplain to Charles Stewart and also to the forces. Not surprisingly when Bovey fell to Parliament he was ousted from his living but not before he made one last defiant gesture. Before leaving he managed to hide one of the church's most valuable possessions, its Elizabethan chalice, and also the parish registers. It is also said that he saved the lectern by dropping it into a pond. When, years later, the restoration came and Charles II ascended the throne, the vicar triumphantly returned after an absence of fifteen years. Given these facts It is not surprising therefore that within the church there is a carving of the coat of arms of Charles II to commemorate the event.

The fact that the report on the battle was written at Ashburton, as indeed so too was an update on the situation at Okehampton, it is worth examining Asburton's role during the Civil War.

Ashburton

Like Chagford, mentioned earlier, Ashburton has a long history having been one of the county's ancient stannary towns and having held a market for some eight hundred years. A number of old buildings can still be found and those who use the town centre car park will find themselves using an ancient, narrow and hump-backed bridge more suited to pack horses than the modern motor car. The River Yeo which flows beneath was once known as the 'Ashburn' from which the town derives its name.

With all the Civil War activity which occurred at nearby Bovey Tracy one could perhaps expect some effects to have been felt at Ashburton. Indeed there was contact between opposing forces although this seems to have been minor and brief. A report to Parliament after the battle of Bovey gives us an insight of what happened. It reads:

"The Army advanced the next day being Saturday to Ashburton, but the enemy having received a hot alarm by those that escaped, quit that place being their head-quarter, in great confusion sending their foot one way and their horse another way. Our forlorn hope pursued then so fast through Ashburton that we took twenty horse and nine prisoners. This day the General advances to Totnes where the enemy hath a Foot-quarter but just now Intelligence is come that they have quit the Town."

Evidence of Parliament's occupation of the town following the above report can be seen today in Broad Street very close to the centre of town, known locally as the 'Bullring'. A shop close to its junction with East and West Streets will be instantly recognisable as an ironmongers for frequently its wares are displayed outside. The shop is also distinctive for its pointed stone archway beyond which is a heavy door, visual evidence of its great age. However, it has not always been an ironmongers and in the 17th Century would have been the scene of much merriment and drinking for this was once the 'Mermaid Inn'.

Today a plaque above the arch tells passersby of its Civil War connection and how General Fairfax stayed there after the Battle of Bovey.

The archway of the former Mermaid Inn

The Teign Valley

After leaving Ashburton it would seem that Faixfax and his troops had the intention of moving southwards towards Totnes. However, before we do so too it is worth spending a short while exploring Civil War activity in upper reaches of the Teign Valley where we begin with a mystery at Christow.

Christow

Lying on the steep western slopes of the Teign Valley is the village of Christow which at first glance appears too small to have been of much interest to either side during the Civil War. Today the war will be far from visitors' minds as they come to the area to visit Canonteign

Falls, reputedly England's highest waterfall although, In fairness to other contenders, what it may gain in height it lacks in breadth. There are other leisure activities in the park whilst nearby is Canonteign House which was built in 1812 to replace old Canonteign House, a beautiful Tudor mansion, situated a short distance away. Neither building is open to the public but it is the old Tudor mansion, now carefully restored, which is the centre of our first incident.

In 1645 old Canonteign House was held by the royalists who it has been said turned it into a small fortress. Despite that, however, it still fell to an assault by parliamentary forces led by Fairfax. Although access is prohibited one can see sufficient of the building from the narrow public road passing close to its western elevation to understand why it would be so valuable as a strategic base above the valley. In the village itself we find a mystery which centres on the parish church.

One can read a number of books on the Civil War and frequently the story of Nicholas Busell will crop up. It is told as thus:

"Elderly Nicholas Busell was the local church warden and daily went about the tasks he had performed for the past forty-six years. He knew churches were a frequent target for roundhead soldiers who, given the chance, would plunder the silver plate and other items of value. One can therefore imagine his horror when he emerged from the dark interior of the church and, locking the door behind him, saw a posse of roundheads staring at him in the sunlight, their muskets and pistols at the ready. He was immediately ordered to unlock the door to facilitate their entry but he stubbornly refused. No one was going to defile his beloved church, either cavalier or roundhead. An ultimatum was given, either hand over the keys or be shot. He refused, a pistol shot rang out and he died on the spot."

In honour of his many years of service to the church, and the sacrifice he had made, Nicholas Busell was buried where he fell. To find the spot one has to look no further than one's feet as one enters the church. The slab of his tomb will be underfoot.

The grave of Nicholas Busell

It is a story which makes interesting reading so what is the mystery? One can visit the church and see the grave. The inscription on the stone is becoming a little worn now with the passing of so many years but nevertheless can still be deciphered. The date of his death is shown as 1631 whereas the Civil War did not begin until more than a decade later. What is the answer? Are the stories of him being shot by roundheads unfounded or was the date of the death recorded wrongly, perhaps if the inscription was renewed at a later date. Perhaps he did die in 1631 and was shot as told, except that it was not by roundheads but ordinary robbers. A leaflet in the church refers to the incident but gives no hint of the true answer.

Ashton

From Christow cross the River Teign by way of a narrow stone bridge, originally built in 1604, and follow the signs for Ashton. These twin villages, comprising Lower and Higher Ashton, stretch from the river valley to the lower western slopes of the Haldon Hills and was once the ancestral home of the Chudleigh family. Prominent as commanders during the Civil War, they have already been mentioned in connection with Bideford Fort and the Battle of Sourton.

To understand events which were to occur at Higher Ashton it is necessary to know a little of the Chudleigh family history at the time of the Civil War. To begin with both father and son were parliamentarians and whilst both were military commanders it was the son, James Chudleigh, who was the brilliant tactician and routed Hopton's army at Sourton in April, 1643. These two were to meet again, however, a few weeks later when, on the 16th May, there were to fight a ferocious battle at Stratton in North Cornwall. This time the tables were turned.

Being in Cornwall, and outside of the area covered by this book, it is suffice to say that Hopton took over 1700 prisoners and recaptured all the weapons he had previously lost plus seventy barrels of gunpowder and £5,000 in cash. Amongst those captured was James Chudleigh who had been left abandoned with his troops when the overall parliamentary commander, Lord Stamford, fled.

Chudleigh became a scapegoat for the defeat and no doubt sensing a feeling of injustice he changed sides to fight for the royalist cause. In fairness this was something which frequently happened during the Civil War and was not only limited to men of one side. However, the fact that his son had now been branded a traitor by Cromwell was too much for his father and he, too, declared his loyalty to the Crown. Given these facts it was not surprising that, when in the area, Cromwell would pay their ancestral home a visit.

This visit came in 1645 when their home at Place Barton was besieged by roundheads. The royalist defenders were not in a strong position and there is little evidence that the siege was other than a short one. There is a report that some damage was done to the door but no trace of this remains.

Place Barton still exists as a working farm although the fine old manor house lies out of public gaze obscured by a high wall and farm buildings. In private ownership, the occupants' privacy should be respected.

This ancient gateway at Place Barton can be seen from the road

The manor lies in the shadow of Ashton's 15th Century parish church which sits high on the side of a hill and it is here we can actually see evidence of the ravages of war. Two paths lead from the road to the churchyard, the first of which is rather steep and leads directly to the lych gate whilst the second, a turning further up the hill, is a narrow cobbled path which takes one past a pair of attractive cob and thatch cottages to enter the churchyard through a small gate at their rear. Either path will bring you to the solid west door.

Before entering the church study the door carefully and you will see evidence of bullet holes, some of which have penetrated the woodwork completely, some only partially. More effective is to see the holes from inside the church where one is conscious of the light coming through.

One of the bullet holes in Ashton Church door showing how
the force of the penetrating bullet was sufficient to splinter
the wood on the inside of the door

From Higher Ashton we return to recross the ancient bridge over the River Teign and follow the road through the valley southwards so as to eventually reach Newton Abbot.

Newton Abbot

Historically, Newton Abbot's crowning glory is Forde House. This fine Jacobean mansion was built in 1610 by a Richard Reynell and his daughter was later to marry one of Cromwell's military commanders, General Waller. In more peaceful times, prior to the outbreak of the Civil War, it is known that King Charles stayed at the house on at least two occasions and during one of them Richard Reynell was knighted. When the Civil War came Forde House, like so many great houses, changed sides at least once. Originally occupied by sympathisers of the King, it was later taken over by Parliament which, given the family connections with General Waller, is perhaps not surprising. However, this was not a fortified house and it is understood no great damage was done.

Some years later, in 1688, when William Prince of Orange landed at Brixham with a small army to take the throne as William III, it was at Forde House that he spent his first night on English soil.

The front facade of the house, seen above, is easily visible from the main road as it leads out of the town towards Torquay. It lies on the left, beyond wide lawns and today is owned by the Teignbridge District Council who have erected new office accommodation to the rear. Access is via Brunel Road and for information on visits it is advisable to contact the council offices.

Compton Castle

Mention was made earlier of the report which stated that the _"General advances towards Totnes where the enemy hath a Foot-quarter"_ whilst a later addendum said that _"... Just now Intelligence is come, they have quit the town."_ There appears to be little or no record of any Civil War activity in Totnes beyond that just mentioned but there is evidence that Parliament turned its attention to Compton Castle which is but a few miles away. Apart from Totnes Castle, which is known to have never participated in any conflict, this was the only royalist stronghold in the area capable of resisting Cromwell.

The castle, shown here, was originally built as a manor in 1329 by Geoffrey Gilbert and later enlarged around 1450 before being fortified some seventy years later, reputedly because of French raids on Plymouth and Fowey.

One of the more famous members of the family during its dominant period was Sir Humphrey who is credited with colonising Newfoundland in 1583, only to perish at sea shortly afterwards. The family was also linked to Sir Walter Raleigh who was a half-brother.

Enquiries at the castle failed to discover any significant connections with the Civil War mainly because many records pertaining to the castle were seemingly lost when it commenced its slide into ruin during the 18th Century and the sale by the Gilberts in 1800. It is believed, however, that there was some damage caused during a skirmish there and mention was made of one of the walls being affected. The only corroborative evidence was the fact that a number of cannon balls similar to those used during the Civil War were found nearby.

Today the castle is still occupied by a member of the Gilbert family although now the care of the National Trust. Outside of the winter months it usually opens to the public on three days a week.

The South Hams

Moving westwards we enter an area known as the South Hams. Geographically it covers the coast and hinterland which lies between the Dart and Yealm rivers and is noted for its unspoiled scenery. Totnes lies on its fringe whilst other interesting towns include Dartmouth, Salcombe and Modbury. Each had a part to play in the Civil War and we begin with Dartmouth.

Dartmouth

At the outbreak of the Civil War in 1642 Dartmouth immediately allied itself with the views of Parliament and in doing so became a target for royalist forces. These arrived in 1643 under the command of Prince Maurice, the King's nephew and, finding the town had built substantial defences, laid siege to it. The local population held out for a month before capitulating and after it fell the royalists immediately tightened their grip on it. With access to the English Channel and a fine anchorage it provided an excellent base from which to receive supplies by sea. For the next three years the royalists built up their garrison in expectation of a counterattack by Cromwell's troops. Sir Henry Carey was put in charge of defending Kingswear Castle on the east bank of the river whilst Sir Hugh Pollard took over Dartmouth Castle. Recent research also suggests that the ancient camp at Gallants Bower, above Dartmouth Castle, was strengthened and armed with cannon at this time. It is estimated that royalist forces eventually numbered over two thousand men and 120 cannon, with most of them and the armament based on the strongholds of the castle and Gallants Bower.

Today, children play on cannon at Dartmouth Castle

91

The anticipated assault by Parliament did not come until the latter stages of the war, on the 18th January, 1646, when roundheads stormed in from the north. Resistance melted when Fairfax promised all lives would be spared provided they gave up their arms, ammunition and food supplies. The town surrendered.

Within Dartmouth today are a number of buildings which were in existence at the time of the war, notably the 17th century Butterwalk in the town centre. Here the row of shops have overhanging frontages supported by granite pillars. Also in existence was the castle which predates these events by at least a century and then there is Gallants Bower.

Now in the care of the National Trust, Gallants Bower is creating much local interest because it has only recently been rediscovered. Categorised as a 'major find' this is because it is one of the very few Civil War earthwork forts known to have survived. In this case survival was due to it becoming overgrown for some three centuries and left undisturbed until recently when, realising the significance of the site, the National Trust began the painstaking process of clearing and restoration.

The history of the site is still not altogether clear and research by local historians tends to indicate that it was probably in use, although not necessarily in its final form, prior to the Civil War. Its name certainly predates that era and is said to be a corruption of 'Galions Boure', the name by which it was known as long ago as 1463 when the site was used as a lookout for spotting enemy shipping although whether there were also earthworks there is still not certain. There is a school of thought which tends to think that as it was not mentioned in records as the town built up its defences at the commencement of the war it was probably built later when the royalists arrived and strengthened their garrison. Some of the hardships faced by the men defending this isolated position is graphically portrayed in an account given later by an old soldier who was there. Lying on the ground in the sub-zero temperatures of a January night he had become so frostbitten that his hand had to be amputated.

Salcombe

Worth a mention here is the history of Salcombe Castle or, to give its officially recorded name, Fort Charles. Today the ruins of this former fort will be found on low rock to the east of Salcombe's North Sands beach. It has suffered from sea erosion over a long period of time but steps towards conserving what is left of the structure are in hand.

Early records tend to confirm it was built around the mid-16th Century, at about the same time as the other coastal defences were erected in the area although, unlike those, it was to suffer early abandonment. However, it was destined to have a new lease of life, albeit a temporary one, during the Civil War when, in 1643, Prince Maurice ordered Sir Edmund Fortescue to rebuild it. On completion he renamed it Fort Charles in honour of the King.

By 1646 the forces of Parliament were dominant in the South West and as we read earlier in the January of that year Dartmouth fell to them. At the same time Fairfax's troops laid siege to Fort Charles. It was the 15th January and the royalists were to hold out in their waterside stronghold until the 7th May when, short of supplies, they finally surrendered. Records show its compliment at that time to be sixty-six men. The fort was subsequently occupied until around 1654 when it was rendered useless and abandoned.

Today the site on which it stands is privately owned and there is no public access. Nevertheless, views of it are possible from North Sands Beach.

Modbury

To the west lies the small but old town of Modbury where today its steep main street doubles as the A379 main road between Plymouth and the South Hams. An elevated pavement along one side adds character to a place which already has an interesting blend of architecture, small shops and old inns from various eras. Two battles are recorded as having been fought here, both during the Civil War. The site of the major one is about a mile to the east of the town, just south of a minor road which leads to Aylestone Cross. County records give Its location at O.S. Map 202/665513 and the date as 1643. There is no visible marker at the site, only rolling countryside with a scenic blend of hills and valleys.

Neither the Ordnance Survey nor the county's record of battle sites give the location of the second battle so one must assume it was of lesser importance. It is likely, however, that it was fought near the former Champernowne Estate and Runaway Lane. The reasons for this supposition are twofold. It is known that the Champernowne family fortunes were at their height during the reigns of Henry VIII and Elizabeth I and that they suffered badly during the Civil War when, because of their loyalty to the Crown, their manor was attacked by parliamentary troops and burnt. It was subsequently abandoned and completely demolished in 1705. Apparently it was an outcome which was much favoured by the local inhabitants for they were on the side of Parliament.

The second indicator is based to some extent on local folklore and the name, Runaway Lane, gives a clue as to what happened for it was along here that the royalists fled and were killed after the battle. In fact when the story was discussed, one local added, "*Yes, and they were running backwards!*" But that is not all for, according to the locals, the ghosts of the slain cavaliers still haunt the spot.

If you want to check the story for yourself you will find Runaway Lane located off Church Lane, at the western approach to Modbury. It lies about a hundred yards in from the Church Lane junction with the main road and is on the right. It is unsigned except for a footpath marker near the start. It is reasonably wide here but soon narrows as it rapidly descends a steep slope and one word of warning .... wear stout boots. Runaway Lane has been described as "the wettest lane in Modbury !"

West Devon

Finally, we reach West Devon but before we end at Plymouth there are two more calls to make. Both are on the fringe of Dartmoor, the first stop being at Tavistock and the second at its smaller neighbour, Lydford.

Tavistock

Tavistock is a market town rich in history and owes much of its early prosperity to its once powerful abbey which has been mentioned under the Reformation. It is also synonymous with the Duke of Bedford and one soon finds Bedford Square and the Bedford Hotel. It was a later holder of the title who was to play a role in the town's fortunes during the Civil War. Although his ancestors had much for which to thank the Crown he felt it served his interests to support Parliament. From contemporary reports, however, it seems he did not have an easy time. The town is said to have changed hands no fewer than six times!

In late 1642 the royalist army under Sir Ralph Hopton first took Launceston for the Crown before moving on Tavistock which, at the time, was occupied by parliamentary troops commanded by a Colonel Robert Savery. It seems he beat an orderly retreat and Hopton's forces moved in, one of their first acts being to attack the home of Sir John Maynard. He was an eminent lawyer and also a supporter of Parliament. A contemporary report states that, after destroying all his papers, the troops 'cut his bed to pieces, casting abroad the feathers and pulled down part of the roof of his house.' Apparently the house was never repaired.

A couple of months later, in January 1643, a large force of parliamentary troops under the command of the Earl of Stamford reoccupied the town, Hopton and his army having left for a campaign elsewhere. However, before the month was out Hopton returned and Tavistock changed hands for the third time in as many months. It now became the headquarters for a royalist army under the command of Sir John Berkeley. For the next two months there were a number of skirmishes between opposing sides until, in March 1643, it appears they agreed a local truce. It lasted a month!

With the exception of a short period in the summer of 1644, Tavistock was to remain occupied by royalist forces between May, 1643, and March, 1646. Its brief spell under parliamentary control started on Tuesday, 23rd July, 1644, when roundheads under the Earl of Essex entered the town. One of the first victims on this occasion was Sir Richard Grenville who had once been a commander for Parliament but had defected to the Crown. It was, therefore, no real surprise that Essex would seek him out. It is said, however, that Sir Richard had heard of their intention and by the time the roundheads reached his house on the outskirts of town he had already fled. His staff were left to face the enemy which they did, reputedly, with a white flag flying from the building.

It seems that the white flag had little effect for reports say the roundheads fired shots into the walls and then stormed in. The following extract taken from a report written at the time describes some of the pillage which occurred once entry had been gained.

"... provided excellent pillage for the soldiers, even at least £3000 in money and plate, and other provisions in great quantity, two cannon and there was a room full of excellent good new muskets and many pairs of pistols, as good as can be bought for the money ..."

The stay of Essex and his roundheads was short and ended on the 5th September when King Charles arrived. It was a great day for the town and the first time it had hosted a reigning monarch. He stayed at the town house of the Glanville family and although there are few sites remaining in the town today which can he directly associated with the Civil War this is one of them. The house itself has disappeared but the arched entrance can still be seen in Pym Street, only a minute's stroll from Bedford Square.

By 1646 fortunes were turning strongly in favour of Parliament and in March of that year Tavistock was to change sides once more and for the last time. It had turned full circle and was once more back under Parliament and the side which the majority of the local population had supported. For Tavistock the Civil War had been an eventful period although no great battles were fought there neither was there any great damage to property.

One writer perhaps sums up Tavistock's position when he succinctly describes it as *"...that of a doormat, put there for the convenience of those passing through !"*

Lydford

Lying about eight miles north of Tavistock, on the edge of Dartmoor and within sight of its highest peak, is the long straggling village of Lydford. Here the waters of the Lyd, fast flowing from its source high on the moors, have cut the famous Lydford Gorge. Now owned by the National Trust, it is one of the 'musts' on the tourist trail. However, today's perception of this sleepy village can be deceptive for this was once one of the county's most powerful boroughs and its prison one of England's most notorious. So powerful were the ancient tinners here that they were permitted their own courts, also known as parliaments, and between the 12th and 16th Centuries Lydford reigned supreme.

Living was hard and a tinner's life was short. They lived by a harsh code and transgressors could expect little mercy. A record shows that in 1195 the sum of £75 was spent on building a 'strong house' to detain those offending against the local laws. The original building was two stories high and around fifty feet square then, sometime during the 13th Century, further height was added together with a ditch and mound.

Treatment of offenders can only be described as 'barbaric' and Lydford's prison struck terror into all. Below ground level was a pit, reached only by ladder, and it was here that prisoners were left to starve and rot. In 1510 the Plympton MP, a Richard Strode, is reputed to have described it as "one of the most heinous, contagious and detestable places within this realm."

Like most strongholds within Devon, Lydford's prison did not escape attention during the Civil War although this time, with its role as a prison, it was viewed in a different perspective. When the war started it was placed in the charge of Sir Richard Grenville, a royalist and one of the King's commanders in the West.

Many roundhead prisoners were to die there and one of the many who did was a Colonel James Hals. Hals was visited by a friend, William Browne of Tavistock, who was to become renowned for his poetry. One of his most lasting and poignant pieces relates to the prison's inhumanity. He wrote:

"I oft have heard of Lydford Law,
How in the morn they hang and draw
And sit in judgment after.
At first I wondered at it much,
But since I've found the matter such
That it deserves no laughter.

They have a castle on a hill,
I took it for an old windmill,
The vanes blown off by weather;
To lie therein one night 'tis guessed
'Twere better to be stoned and pressed
Or hanged. Now choose you whether."

There are many more verses to the poem which was written by Browne in 1644 and it was not long after his visit that the prison's last official execution by hanging took place. The identity of that poor soul is not known but there is a record of a Walter Yelland being starved to death there. He was described as a *"Faithful soldier of the Commonwealth who died by the inhumane dealing of the enemy."*

Within fifty years the castle was falling into ruin. Today the infamous keep, or stronghold, still remains perched on top of its grassy knoll. Carefully preserved by English Heritage, entrance is free and possible at all times.

Finally, in this chapter, we come to the county's largest city, Plymouth.

Plymouth

There is so much which could be written about Plymouth's turbulent past, starting with its early days when, like so many settlements along the Devon coast, it had been plundered on many occasions by the Danes. Later, in 1404 and during the Hundred Year's War with France, it was raided again. This time it was by Bretons who, by the time they sailed for home, had left an estimated six hundred homes ablaze. It was also a city which, in the 16th Century, became associated with all the great seamen of the first Elizabethan era and the story of Drake has already been told. In many ways it was these links with the sea which were to determine Plymouth's survival during the Civil War.

Plymouth had come out in strong support of Parliament right from the start. For the royalists the capture and control of a city of such size and importance would be a huge prize for the King and really sums up Plymouth's role in the war. Parliament quickly erected barricades around the city which, in turn, the royalist army tried to penetrate but always without any success. Plymouth's great advantage was its link to the sea. Cromwell had control of the navy and one of the country's greatest admirals, Robert Blake, was in command. As a result their Plymouth garrison was always supplied in time from the sea. When Blake eventually died, having ensured Britain's supremacy at sea, it is said his heart was buried at home in Plymouth whilst his body rests in Westminster Abbey.

To capture some of Plymouth's atmosphere during the Civil War visit the city's famous Hoe. Casting an eye towards the East and the mouth of the Plym as it enters Plymouth Sound, one should see Mount Batten. This ancient fort has enjoyed a military presence right up until the 1990's when finally, the last unit of the Armed Forces, a Royal Air Force maritime unit, moved out. It may surprise some to know that it did not get its name from the royal Mountbattens of current times but is said to have been named after a Captain Batten who was in charge of its defence for Parliament during the Civil War.

Rising peacefully from the waters of the Sound is Drake's Island. Once a fortress, it was used as a prison during the Civil War. Looking towards the city and the Hoe from there, one of the dominant buildings one sees is the Citadel. This massive fortress is still a military barracks but, surprisingly, was not erected until after the Civil War. Even so, there is a link with events of a decade earlier. The restoration of the monarchy saw Charles II ascend the throne in 1660 and one of his first acts was to order the erection of the citadel. It is said that his purpose was twofold. The first was the defence of Plymouth Sound whilst the second was more subtle. The King was well aware of the anti-monarchist sympathies of the city during the Civil War and of its ability to withstand the royalist forces for over three years. It will be seen that the Citadel not only looks seawards but inland over the city as well. As one contemporary commentator said, "it was built as a menace to the rebellious townsmen."

Perhaps, however, Plymouth's role in the Civil War can best be experienced by paying a visit to Freedom Park. Here, with views towards the sea, a large monument marks the site of the last decisive battle on Plymouth soil. It was fought on the 5th December, 1643, and became known as the 'Sabbath Day Fight'. Inscriptions on the huge granite block record events with the following appearing on one side:

"Upon this spot on December 5th 1643, after hard fighting for several days the Roundhead Garrison of Plymouth made their final rally and routed the Cavalier army which had surprised the outworks and well nigh taken the town.

For many years it was the custom to celebrate the anniversary of this victory long known as the 'Sabbath Day Fight' , and recorded as the 'Great Deliverance' of the protracted siege successfully sustained by the troops and townsfolk on behalf of Parliament against the King under great hardship for more than three years."

Two other faces of the memorial briefly record the names of the respective military commanders. One side is inscribed "General for the King - Prince Maurice" whilst the other records "For Parliament - Colonel Wardlaw."

The Civil War monument in Plymouth's Freedom Park

It is not possible to leave the city, however, without briefly mentioning Fort Resolution. This was a bastion during the long siege and on ancient maps of Plymouth was shown as 'Resolution Fort' and standing at the northeast corner of the defensive wall around the city. Lost for ages beneath the former Friary railway station and goods yard, it was rediscovered in the early 1990's whilst redevelopment of the yard was being undertaken and arrangements were made for its preservation. Unfortunately, the remnant is not large, just a right-angled section of the bastion's stone wall retaining a small piece of grassy mound. New brickwork has been added to the top to provide additional support.

Those wishing to find this small remnant of Plymouth history can do so within the Friary Park housing development on the north side of the business park. Enter the estate from Beaumont Road and follow through to the arched building at the end. The remains of Fort Resolution are on the left immediately after passing through the arch. Sadly, at the time of writing the authorities have not yet placed a plaque identifying it. Those not wishing to enter the estate may see part of the wall through railing in Beaumont road although the view is not quite so effective. A copy of a 17th Century map showing the fort's location is reproduced below.

Plymouth at the time of the Civil War
Resolution Fort is shown on the top right section of the city wall

99

Still remaining within the modern city boundary, we cross the River Plym to enter Plympton which, because it was once a town older and more important than Plymouth, deserves its own heading.

Plympton.

Plympton is really two towns rolled into one with Plympton St Mary the more modern and commercial heart whilst Plympton St Maurice is by far the older and, in its day, the more important. Indeed, it has been said that it was a thriving town when Plymouth was merely a hamlet called Sutton. Even then Sutton's lands belonged to the Plympton Priory of St. Peter and St. Paul which was founded by a nephew of William the Conqueror. Arguably its most favourite son, the great portrait painter Sir Joshua Reynolds, was born there in 1723 whilst his father was both vicar and master of the local grammar school and between 1295 and 1832 the town returned its own Member of Parliament.

From the mention of Parliament it is only a short step to the Civil War and the role played by Plympton Castle. This Norman stronghold has already been mentioned earlier in respect of the role played by Baldwin de Redvers its owner at the time of the revolt against King Stephen. The town grew up around its motte and bailey, capped by a keep and sturdy walls, but its fortunes changed. Although rendered militarily useless after the loss to King Stephen it was later rebuilt only to change hands and fall into disrepair again.

By 1642 there were few fortifications left although its strategic elevated position remained. This was sufficient reason for Prince Maurice to garrison his royalists troops there whilst he made a headquarters in Plympton. It is also likely that at least some of the planning for the siege of Plymouth was conducted here. However, as Parliament's military supremacy grew, so the castle at Plympton became one of its victims. Whether it was by siege or battle is not known but in 1644 roundheads under the command of the Earl of Essex took possession of it for Parliament. Since then the ruins have survived and today, set in an open grassy park, are open to the public at any time.

Chapter Six

THE MONMOUTH REBELLION

The Civil War over, Charles I was beheaded in 1649 and a Commonwealth was declared with Oliver Cromwell as the Lord Protector. When he died in 1658 the role passed briefly to his son, Richard, until the monarchy was restored in 1660 with Charles II. When Charles died in 1685 he was succeeded by James II and the West Country was once more plunged into turmoil with the ill-fated 'Monmouth Rebellion'.

Often thought by many to be part of the Civil War, the rebellion in fact occurred almost forty years later. Whilst Devon saw little in the way of action in this ill-fated uprising it did nevertheless play a role. Many local men, particularly from the east of the County, joined the rebel army which, in its early stages, marched through Devon's eastern towns and villages. Later they were to pay a heavy penalty for their actions when they came face to face with the 'hanging judge', Judge Jefferies, and his 'Bloody Assizes'.

As so often in the past, religion was to play an important part in this West Country rebellion. After the restoration of the monarchy King Charles II reigned for twenty-five years but in the later years of his reign there was disquiet as many of the religious and political freedoms gained during the days of the Commonwealth were slowly being eroded away. Indeed, many who professed the Protestant faith were debarred from office. Under the laws of succession which existed when Charles died, the throne passed to his brother, James.

The accession of James II only made matters worse for he was a staunch Catholic and had many friends in France. He quickly tried to consolidate his own position and became a fierce opponent of the Whig Party in Parliament. The Whigs in turn were becoming increasingly worried about the King's autocratic behaviour and started to look for an alternative monarch, finding their likely saviour in James, Duke of Monmouth. He was the eldest illegitimate son of Charles II and had been born in Rotterdam during the time of his father's exile.

He had a reputation for being a good military commander but, more importantly, was a Protestant. It did not take much persuasion for the Duke to set sail for England where he had been advised an 'army' awaited his arrival.

On the 11th June, 1685, the 'invasion' began when a fleet of three ships, carrying a force of just over eighty men, sailed into Lyme Bay and anchored off the Cobb at Lyme Regis. His choice of Lyme is said to have been due to two reasons. Firstly, he had received a warm welcome in the West Country during a tour a few years earlier and felt the local population would be sympathetic to his cause and, secondly, he had been told the fort guarding Lyme was armed with five cannon which he was confident he could take and thus enlarge his own arsenal. Unfortunately, whilst his strategy was correct he did not know they were without gunpowder!

Landing on the beach the Duke unfurled his banner for all to see his motto: "Fear Nothing but God". He then knelt in prayer. It is said that personally Monmouth had no great aspirations for the throne, only to see the Protestant religion defended and the French influence at Court stopped. He hoped, too, to persuade James II to accept the dominance of Parliament and for himself to be welcomed at court. Furthermore, as a military man, he hoped to be made commander of the army. James II, of course, had other ideas.

Having made his position secure at Lyme Regis, the Duke quickly increased the size of his army which soon numbered over two thousand. Then, on 15th June, 1685, he left Lyme with his motley army of poorly armed, ill-prepared and undisciplined west countrymen. Within a mile they had crossed into Devon and were heading northwards through Uplyme before continuing to Axminster.

It has been said that Monmouth's army initially advanced at such great speed that it put fear into the King's local militia to an extent that many of the men deserted and joined the rebels. By the time Axminster was reached it is estimated the rebels had grown by another thousand to become three thousand strong. Of these five hundred were described as 'scythe men' and armed with devastatingly sharp curved weapons. Others carried an assortment of similar farming implements to such an extent that the uprising now became more popularly known as 'The Pitchfork Rebellion'.

Axminster welcomed the Duke and there is no report of any battle on Devon soil. The real fighting was to come later. As the rebel army grew so did the alarm in London. Lord Churchill, later to become Duke of Marlborough, was ordered posthaste to the West Country with a mixed force of cavalry comprising Horse Guards and Dragoons, the latter being mounted infantry armed with short muskets. Churchill hoped to catch Monmouth before he left Lyme but he arrived two days late. Monmouth had left for Axminster. Churchill followed and occupied Axminister but by then Monmouth was in Taunton.

From there on all the action for the Monmouth, or Pitchfork, Rebellion took place outside of Devon. Monmouth's ragged army was finally defeated at the Battle of Sedgemoor, near Bridgwater in Somerset, on the 6th July ,1685. Over seven hundred rebels were killed, many of them Devon men. The death toll amongst the King's troops was twenty-seven!

A portrait of the Duke of Monmouth who was popular in the West Country

James, Duke of Monmouth, escaped but was later captured and charged with treason. He was executed on London's Tower Hill on the 15th July. His ill-fated rebellion had lasted barely a month.

In the West Country the fate of his supporters was equally merciless. Enquiries were made as to whom had been absent from home or work during the time of the rebellion and immediately suspicion fell on those who had. It has been estimated that probably around a thousand men from East Devon alone had been absent, with a further three thousand from Dorset and Somerset adding to the numbers. The authorities were keen to make examples of them all.

In the autumn of 1685 the Lord Chief Justice, Judge Jefferies, was given the task of organising the trials of the rebels and one of the venues for his Autumn Assize was Exeter. These infamous events became known as the 'Bloody Assizes' due to the fact that the death penalty was more often than not given to all those who pleaded 'not guilty', with execution being almost immediate.

Even death was not necessarily the end for, as was so often the case in those days, the corpses were dismembered and parts of their bodies distributed for public hanging in the towns and villages as a warning to others. In fact, it is reputed that many remained hanging until the landing of William, Prince of Orange, at Brixham three years later. On taking the throne he ordered that the bodies be removed and given decent burials. Until then one commentator said that the West Country resembled a butcher's shop!

Although there are no sites in Devon which can be visited as being specifically part of the Monmouth Rebellion, it is known that one of the venues for the series of 'Bloody Assizes' was Exeter. Until the mid-20th century Exeter's ancient Guildhall was the location for all local assizes so it seems more than likely that this is where they were held when Judge Jefferies came to town.

Chapter Seven

THE 18th and 19th CENTURIES

INDUSTRIAL, BREAD and RELIGIOUS RIOTS

The 18th Century was not without turmoil and rioting was frequent. The causes of fighting were various but mainly they were over working conditions and the cost of food, often the two being interrelated. The workers expected to be able to purchase essential everyday commodities at a 'fair price' and when merchants were seen as profiteers the result was often violence. One commentator of the day described Devon as bordering on a state of anarchy!

The reasons for these problems were many. The population was growing whereas food production was not keeping pace with demand, a problem made worse by the failure of a number of harvests. The net result was rising food prices whilst the workers' wages remained static. When the workers weren't rioting against the price of food then it was against their employers on a matter of pay. With one of the mainstays of the Devonshire economy being the wool trade it was not surprising that many of the disputes involved workers in that industry and one of the 18th century's earliest recorded outbreaks focused on the county's weavers. In November, 1717, in a widespread display of anger, over a thousand weavers gathered together to rampage through numerous local towns slashing cloth, destroying looms and damaging stores. Three years later, in 1720, trouble erupted again. In fact, during the last decade of the 18th Century, the 1790s, there were forty-one recorded riots in the county! But any thoughts that the 19th Century would bring peace to Devon were only illusory. Furthermore, there was unease at the way the military were being used to quell civilian unrest and even the Lord Chief Justice of the day expressed his concern. Often, too, the soldiers were in sympathy with the rioters and deliberating fired high to avoid injuries. As a result magistrates frequently refused to read the Riot Act which usually heralded the military's arrival.

However, besides industrial unrest there were a number of other causes of public disquiet such as the price of staple commodities, for example bread, and also on occasion religious intolerance. Here we look at some of the local events as they occurred in both centuries. They are, however, described in geographical order rather than in any chronological sequence or for the reasons behind them.

Tiverton's Industrial and Bread Riots

In the 18th Century Tiverton was a great centre for the local woollen industry so in many ways it was natural that when trouble flared the town would bear the brunt of it. And flare again it did, in 1720. This time, however, the reason was 'imports'. The local clothiers had begun to import Irish wool, much to the anger of the local woolcombers who saw it as a threat to their livelihood. They broke into the clothiers' shops and managed to burn most of the imported wool after a pitched battle with constables. After this incident an uneasy peace descended over the town but tensions were always bubbling just below the surface.

Although the lid stayed on for a further eighteen years, it was no surprise when trouble flared again. It was 1738 and this time the woolcombers' grievance focused on the merchants who were paying their masters such a low price for goods that, in turn, their masters could not pay them a sufficient wage on which to live. As a result they stated their intention of entering Tiverton to destroy merchants' houses. As they approached the town they found their path blocked by a contingent of a hundred special constables. Undeterred, fierce fighting broke out during which one man was killed and the woolcombers managed to force their way past the defensive cordon of constables. Finding themselves helpless and at the mercy of the mob the merchants immediately agreed higher prices before their homes were destroyed. However, not all escaped unscathed and it was reported that one merchant had his stocks of cloth destroyed before being 'horsed on a staff' through the town and unceremoniously dumped in front of Tiverton's mayor. It is said that in this instance the masters condoned their workers' behaviour because it also brought them higher prices too from the merchants. Despite this, however, tension between masters and their workers still remained.

It was a tension which was to surface in Tiverton yet again, this time in 1749 when the main battle was between the woolcombers and the weavers. Initially, the protest began peacefully as a simple strike but, when eventually the woolcombers' funds ran out, violence once more erupted. The cause of the problem this time lay in the fact that the weavers, not wishing to be so dependent upon local wool supplies or upon the local woolcombers, who were now seen as a disruptive force, preferred weaving Irish wool. An uneasy peace was eventually restored in the town but not before the Riot Act had been read and the military called in to restore order. The clothiers offered to cut their supplies from Ireland but this did not satisfy the woolcombers, many of whom, it is said, decided to leave the area.

It is perhaps interesting to see that over half a century later, after so much turmoil and a serious decline in the wool trade, Tiverton should once more emerge as one of the main centres of the textile industry. Ironically, this change in fortune being due to labour problems elsewhere. It was 1816 and at Loughborough, in Leicestershire,

John Heathcoat was having problems at his factory where he had recently introduced his new invention, a bobbin for lace making. Local *'Luddites'*, fearing a loss of jobs, systematically began breaking all the machines. Finally, frustrated, Heathcoat looked for an alternative site and found it at Tiverton. He never looked back and was to become one of the foremost manufacturers of lace, net and other fine fabrics, the factory employing at its peak some 2500 people.

By the mid-19th Century there was rioting over the price of bread in a number of Devonshire towns and in May, 1847, it was Tiverton's turn to feel the rioters' wrath. Unfortunately, there was little recorded on the police files of the day except for the fact that troops were called in from Exeter to quell the riot and provide assistance to one of their constables and two specials. That local resources were completely inadequate to police the riots was evident from a Government Inspector's report written some twenty years later. It records that the Borough then had a police force of seven men but that the area requiring policing was extensive and the numbers too limited to provide for *"the watching and protection of the district under their charge."*

Honiton's Bread and Religious Riots

One of the earliest recorded disturbances during the 18th Century, which involved rioting over the price of bread, occurred in Honiton in 1766. Here a crowd of workers forcibly took a consignment of corn from local farmers and sold it for what they thought was a fair price. Fortunately, it seems that it ended more or less amicably when the workers gave the proceeds of the sale to the farmers and even, it is said, returned their sacks!

But events were not usually as peaceful and a familiar cry of the rioters was **"we might as well be hanged as starve to death."** And that is often what happened as the alleged ring leader of one such riot at Chudleigh found to his cost. Bread riots occurred throughout the county with major outbreaks in Torquay and Plymouth. Neither did East Devon escape unscathed as these incidents will show.

However, Honiton also sprang to prominence when it became the scene of the first recorded riots in Devon against the newly formed Salvation Army. These were reported on the 21st December, 1882 ,with an account of the disturbance appearing in the 'Devon Weekly Times' the following day. Describing the event as *'serious'* it reported that it had been known the Salvation Army's processions were to be renewed and there was local opposition. The opposing factions of army and locals met in the High Street and there, as well as in the hall, *'an almost indescribable scene occurred.'* The report then continues to describe how stones, flour and other things were thrown in all directions and considerable injury was caused to some Army members. It is said that one of their group had his right eye *'nearly knocked out'* , another received a serious blow to the head whilst Constable Webber, trying to keep order, had a *'nasty cut on the face from which blood flowed freely.'*

But PC Webber was not alone for, expecting trouble, extra police had been drafted into Honiton, although it seems their numbers were totally inadequate. The newspaper reported the mob as being *'immense'* and numbering some two thousand.

The Salvationists' meeting in the hall was constantly disturbed, missiles thrown and at one stage a pistol was discharged. Fortunately, the bullet caused no injury but the incident was sufficient for the police to renew their efforts to restore order and eventually the hall was cleared.

Exmouth's Bread and Military Riots

Simultaneous with major rioting elsewhere on the 5th November, 1867, an outbreak also occurred at Exmouth. Not that this was the town's first incident. That occurred in 1846 but had been a relatively minor protest against the price of bread reaching *"1s 0½p for a 4lb loaf with flour at 15s a bushel."*

However, in 1867 things were different and the authorities sensed that major problems were brewing and had the foresight to swear in fifty special constables to assist the parish constable, one Isaac Rake. Despite these precautions Exmouth was still to suffer a night of violence which the local newspaper, the 'Exmouth Journal', later recalled in an article as being a night when *'the mob held almost unchecked rule over the town's streets.'*

The report went on to describe that there was hardly a baker's or butcher's shop in the town which did not have its windows broken with the shop of a Mr W.S. Clapp on The Strand being particularly badly damaged with doors also being stove in. Only a couple of shops were to escape major damage and in these cases the proprietors promised the rioters they would reduce their prices. It then continued to describe how the rioting was to shake the fabric of Exmouth until three o'clock the following morning with skirmishes between groups of rioters and the specials. The next day a further sixty 'specials' were sworn in to join a contingent of the Coastguard and Naval Reserve which had been drafted in to assist. At seven o'clock the following evening the forces of law and order assembled in The Strand and were able to keep the mob in check.

Thwarted in the town centre, the mob then made their way to vent their anger at the home of a Mr Morey, a baker, who lived in Albion Street. Others made their way to some of the outlying farms but it seems little damage was caused here for the farmers were quick to appease the mob with helpings of bread and cheese, washed down with copious amounts of local cider!

One building at the heart of the baking industry which did not escape so lightly was the Flour Mill at Withycombe. Subsequently repaired, it finally succumbed to serious flooding almost a century later. Today a relic in the form of the old mill's water wheel stands surrounded by flowers at the entrance to Exmouth's Madeira Walk.

Withycombe Mill's water wheel, a survivor of the bread riots

So often we read how, when many riots occurred, the military were called in as a peacekeeping force. But what happens when the military themselves are the cause of the problem? This was something else Exmouth was to discover. Woodbury Common, a wide expanse of heath on the outskirts of the town, has enjoyed a long association with the military and today provides an important training ground for potential Royal Marine Commandos from their base at Lympstone.

During the Second World War it housed Dalditch Camp, also a large Royal Marine base, some remnants of which can still be found among the heather and gorse. However, its use by the military can be traced back as far as the 19th Century when it was regularly used as a summer training ground by a number of regiments and the summer of 1893 was no exception.

Here we look to the late Bill Gorfin, for years the Editor of the 'Exmouth Journal', for an eyewitness account of events. It was July and Bill, then a young lad, recalls that the Exmouth area was inundated with some ten thousand troops. These included members of the South West Volunteer Division and battalions of the Royal Welsh Regiments and the South Wales Borderers. There were early signs of trouble when disgraceful scenes were reported as the troops travelled to the area by train. Apparently they were dismantling automatic vending machines on the platforms as the train stopped at various stations on route to its final destination, the railway station at Exmouth. The scene drew hundreds of local spectators who cheered the men as they marched off through the night to establish their camp at Blackhill on the Common.

Unfortunately, peace was short lived for apparently a number of drinking booths had been set up close to the camp and, after heavily drinking at one of these, a number of soldiers from the South Wales Borderers decided to continue their drinking in Exmouth. It was not surprising, therefore, when Bill Gorfin saw a soldier being dragged and escorted by constables towards the town's police station which was then in South Street. It was a situation which rapidly deteriorated as the prisoner's colleagues tried to release him and whose numbers were swelled by other inebriated soldiers who, in turn, were joined by the more unruly elements of Exmouth life. A number of stones were thrown and a second soldier was arrested. Somehow the police were able to make the comparative safety of the police station but further trouble loomed.

Sensing escalating danger, the officers within the police station quickly barricaded the door, although at one stage it seemed that this alone would be insufficient. The mob outside had somehow commandeered a timber wagon with the intention of using it as a battering ram against the police station door.

Fortunately, before any serious damage could be done, a military picket arrived on the scene. Bill describes them as arriving **"on horseback and with swords drawn."**

Hoping to quickly bring about an end to the confrontation, they asked that the prisoners be released into military custody but the police officers declined saying they did not have the authority to do so. It was a response that did little to ease the situation and the crowd's fury rose. In the end the situation was relieved by a General Rocke, a local magistrate, who ordered the release of the second prisoner. By now the military pickets had been reinforced and almost outnumbered the unruly mob and the glint of steel of their swords became sufficient to make most of them drift away, although not before most of the police station windows had been smashed.

What brought about such a night of violence? Well in this case it seems Exmouth's problems started through what has been described as 'the tactless act of a fussy woman.' A Mrs Sellers, whose husband owned stables opposite the railway station, which incidentally is a site now occupied by an amusement arcade, entered them to find a soldier urinating against the wall. She screamed at him and he, being the worse for drink, swore back whereupon the police were called to effect the arrest Bill Gorfin had seen.

The following day a court was held in the Public Hall in Rolle Street when several men were fined for variously being drunk and disorderly and assaulting the police. The original soldier was fined £1 for being drunk and disorderly and resisting arrest, although his colleague was not let off so lightly. General Rocke, sitting on the Bench, said that the charge of attempting to secure the release of a prisoner by force was far more serious. On behalf of the prisoner, however, much was made of his physical condition for he had appeared in court heavily bandaged and weakened through loss of blood. This, it was alleged, was due to unnecessary force being used during his arrest and subsequently. The General was unsympathetic to this view and sentenced the soldier to fourteen days hard labour in the County Gaol at Exeter.

Apparently, the severity of the sentence drew a large crowd which accompanied the 'black maria' taking the prisoner to the railway station. Tensions still remained in the town but when trouble flared up again it was to be in the normally peaceful village of Woodbury. Here soldiers went on the rampage looting inns and a number of local shops and virtually wrecking the Globe Inn which stood at the top of Globe Hill. However, if you wish to visit the inn today you will be unlucky. It burned down some years ago!

Such was the violence experienced in East Devon in July, 1893, that the War Office reviewed the future military use of Woodbury Common. Whilst it still remains a vital location for military training, apart from a few years during WWII, it has never again seen the numbers which arrived in that fateful summer.

Exeter's Religious and Bread Riots

Like Honiton, Exeter was to suffer from riots sparked by religious intolerance, although in this case the events occurred almost two hundred years earlier. Once again it was the Ship Inn in St. Martin's Lane which was a focus of attention and the following facts were recorded:

It was 1710 and locally a Dr. Henry Sacheverell was on trial for having preached two sermons against the unpopular Whig government. His treatment angered many locals and a mob formed intent on extracting revenge on a number of Whig-sponsored clergy who were believed to be hiding in the Ship Inn. Reputedly an eyewitness reported:

"Certain fellows did drag burning faggots and had like to have burned down the old Ship spite mine host and his musket ... had not soldiers come down and made an end of the fire and very nigh the rioters as well!"

As we have seen earlier there were always rumblings just below the surface and it was therefore not surprising that the bread riots of the mid-nineteenth century did not leave the city unscathed. Like Exmouth, the 5th November, 1867, was to see similar violence erupt in Exeter.

The following day the city's local newspaper, 'The Trewmans' Exeter Evening Post', carried extensive reporting of the rioting, in fact, sufficient to cover several of the papers columns. Some excerpts read as follows:

"For 4 or 5 hours the streets were in the possession of a crowd of perhaps a couple of thousand ruffians who, protesting rather vehemently against the high price of bread and meat, seemed to think that the readiest way to produce a reaction in the markets was the smash the windows of the butchers and bakers and now and then, by way of diversion, to smash the shutters, toss out two or three dozen loaves of bread, and throw a sack of flour to the wind ..."

Surprisingly, it wasn't all men who were causing the mayhem, women were playing their part too as the newspaper also points out in the following passage:

"Tradesmen all want to be gentlemen now, said one of the ringleaders of the mob, a woman, but we'll show them if they get their money one way they'll lose it another."

The article then continued with a list of properties damaged. These extended throughout the city and, reading it, it seems that hardly a street avoided the attentions of the rioters. As far as the authorities were concerned the blame for the rioting was quickly attributed to a young semi-anarchist group known as the 'Young Exeter Party' who, apparently, were renowned for stirring up trouble from time to time.

So how did it end? Well the same newspaper spreads a little light on this when it reported the intervention of the military as follows:

"Captain Gatham came saw and conquered. The sight of those glittering steel bayonets beneath the gas light of the Guildhall chilled the enthusiasm of even the most riotous tempers, and as we write the 20th Regiment are marching through the High Street..."

Certainly, the newspaper's graphic description of troops marching through Exeter's High Street with **bayonets glittering beneath the gas light of the Guildhall** should have been enough to make any protesters have second thoughts about continuing. And indeed it was, for their presence brought to a conclusion an event which had seen a riotous mob of some two thousand persons rampaging through Exeter.

It can be safely assumed that on the 5th November, 1867, Exeter was a *'battlefield'*, if not in a strict military sense then certainly in the minds of its inhabitants.

Exeter Guildhall where in 1867 the army's steel bayonets glittered under its gas lights and brought an end to rioting

Elsewhere in the county there were also bread riots and arguably one of the earliest of these occurred between Chudleigh and Kingsteignton.

Chudleigh's Bread Riot

As we have seen, there were many 'bread riots' in Devon during the mid-19th Century but probably one of the county's earliest occurred in 1795 at the Bella Marsh Mills, near Chudleigh Knighton. A very graphic account of the incident appears in the *'History of the City of Exeter'* and also in *'Out of the Blue'*, a history of the Devon Constabulary which was published on its centenary in 1956. It is worth repeating here for it shows the harshness of the penal system at that time:

"The price of provisions, especially wheat, advancing greatly, created much murmuring and dissatisfaction amongst the common people: who, judging the evil to have arisen from nefarious practices of the opulent millers (whom they suspected of engrossing great quantities of grain) collected in a mob and proceeded to Bella Marsh Mills, Chudleigh, which they partly demolished, plundered the

grain they could find and furiously insulted and ill treated the proprietor, Mr Balle. For this offence one Mr Campion, a Blacksmith, of Drewsteignton, was apprehended as a ringleader, committed to gaol, and on trial, being convicted, was sentenced to be executed near the spot where the crime was committed.

In order to strike terror, and prevent future commotions, the execution was conducted in a manner hitherto unknown in this city, being entirely military and entrusted to the care of Major Shadwell, of the 25th Regiment of Light Dragoons.

The unfortunate man (much pitied) was conducted from the new Gaol to the place of execution in a mourning coach, guarded by the Light Dragoons, the troop of Volunteer Cavalry of Sir Stafford Northcote and Sir John de la Pole, the two companies of Exeter and several other of the neighbouring volunteers; and, in order to prevent a rescue, a battalion of militia, with two field pieces, were ordered to march to the neighbourhood. The execution, which was solemn and peaceable, struck great awe in the minds of the spectators, while the unhappy victim to the law was much lamented, as he had ever bore a good character. He declared he was obliged to leave his work and join the rioters."

As stated, the execution was carried out at the scene of the crime and Campion was hanged at the Mills, in the parish of Kingsteignton.

Although the actual mill was demolished some years ago, the old house, Bellamarsh Barton, still stands and is marked on the Ordnance Survey map. Of great character, its origins lie in the 14th Century. Today, however, it is in private occupation and the owner's privacy should be respected.

Detail of its ancient doorway is shown here and it is probable that the execution took place in the large yard in front of it.

Torquay

Staying in South Devon, those who look upon Torquay as the genteel 'Queen of the English Riviera' are often shocked when they learn it was not always so peaceful. In the past it has been witness to both bread and religious riots. Fortunately for those interested in such events, they have been well recorded.

The First Bread Riots

The first bread riots in the town broke out on Monday, 17th May, 1847, although the event was not altogether unexpected for rumours of an impending riot had been rife for some days. Unfortunately, the authorities did not expect there to be much danger of a riot actually happening so no contingency plans were made. However, the rumours became reality and at 7.30 p.m. on the Monday evening, as though by order, a mob suddenly collected in the town's Lower Union Street. There they immediately attacked the local bakers' shops where, it was reported, the women accompanying the rioters carried off loaves of bread in their aprons.

The problem was heightened by the fact that soon most of this criminal activity was being carried out under the cover of darkness, even though it was in the centre of town. It appears that the local commissioners, short of public funds, had issued an edict that no street lights were to be lit during the summer months and to make sure this order was carried out all the gas burners had been removed. In the ensuing panic an order was given to turn on the gas anyway, notwithstanding the lack of burners, so that the ring leaders could be identified. It is reported that when this was done the street lamps emitted flames up to a foot high!

Shedding light on the riot only added to the dismay of those attempting to restore order for it revealed that the crowd had reached several thousand strong. By now the mob had moved on to Fleet Street where, attacking one shop, they met fierce resistance from its owner. Armed with a crowbar he reputedly dealt the mob's leader a substantial blow to the head which immediately felled him to the ground. It is not reported what subsequently happened to the shopkeeper! Reaching The Strand further shops became in jeopardy but by now some of the shopkeepers were adopting a psychological approach to the danger. Quickly they handed out stocks of bread to the rioters who, in return, refrained from damaging their property.

From The Strand the rioters retraced their steps back through the town towards Torre, reportedly sacking bakers' shops close to where the present police station stands. Here they were met by two Magistrates and a number of the local tradesmen and the Riot Act was read. A small number of arrests were made and the prisoners taken to the town's lockup. At midnight the Magistrates returned to the Town Hall where they commenced to hear the charges. Three of the rioters were committed for trial whilst other offenders were remanded.

At noon the following day the Magistrates were still examining the facts concerning other offenders in custody when a crowd of about sixty angry navvies arrived on the scene. They were employed on the new railway works taking place at Torre and came armed with pick axes and other similar tools. They let the authorities know in no uncertain terms that it was their intention to wreck the Town Hall unless their colleagues were released.

By then, however, relief was under way. A Revenue cutter, the 'Adelaide', and another vessel, the 'Vulcan', brought in detachments of coastguards to restore order and these were joined by some forty men from the 5th Fusiliers. In addition, approximately three hundred special constables were sworn in. With the odds turning against them the rioters dispersed without further trouble.

As Torquay returned to normal so were plans made for the trials of the offenders. A local publication, dated 9th July, 1847, gives the following facts:

Over two hundred and thirty rioters were sentenced to terms of imprisonment. Two principal ring leaders were each transported for ten years whilst a further six were given sentences of seven years for aggravating their part by attempting to forcibly rescue prisoners. Sixty-four received prison terms of a year and a further ten rioters were given six months. For the remaining one hundred and fifty prisoners, sentences ranged from between one week and three months.

Another interesting fact to emerge from this episode is that at one stage the authorities discovered a plot to ambush a coach taking prisoners to Exeter thus facilitating their escape. Alternative transport was arranged and this involved sending them by ship from Torquay to Topsham from where it was only a short journey into Exeter.

A note of the meeting of Quarter Sessions held on the 19th October, 1847, shows that approval was given for the expenditure of £60.7s.9p being the cost of transferring prisoners from Torquay to Exeter after the riot.

Memories were obviously short in Torquay for twenty years later a second wave of rioting was to break out in the town.

The Second Bread Riots

It was the 5th November, 1867, when Torquay's second bread riots broke out and once again the price of a basic commodity, bread, was the cause. Unlike the previous occasion, however, this time the authorities were prepared. By good fortune one of the Magistrates associated with the earlier riots, a Mr H.C.M. Phillips, was the Senior Magistrate and when he received an anonymous letter warning of trouble to come he took immediate action.

This entailed summoning the Volunteer Yeomen to the Town Hall where he explained that under the law as it stood they could only be used to quell military riots. However, he suggested that he swear them in as special constables whereupon they could assist him, albeit only armed with normal police staves and not firearms. They immediately agreed and in no time at all Mr Phillips had a hundred and fifty keen special constables at his disposal. These he divided into squads of thirty men, each with a senior officer in charge and two subalterns. The contingent was to be under his authority as Chief Magistrate and he would issue the orders.

The rioters for their part had picked a good day for mayhem with Guy Fawkes celebrations well under way which included the rolling of tar barrels in the street. The mob needed little encouragement under these conditions and soon provoked a gang of youths to attack a bread shop in Lower Union Street. Although the premises had been shuttered these were soon broken down and the glass behind smashed. The contents of the shop were then thrown into the street. During the evening many other properties were reported as having been destroyed or seriously damaged, it even being said that women were used to bring down heavy stones from the Ellacombe area of the town. These were then used by the rioters as ammunition against the newly sworn in special constables. It was further reported that several were badly injured and that even the Chief Magistrate was amongst the victims. It is said that he was struck with such violence that it caused disfigurement to the side of his face. Despite the odds, the constables stood their ground and the legal formality of reading the Riot Act was performed. The ingenuity of some of the rioters is revealed in the following account extracted from the records:

Unlike twenty years previously, this time the street lights were in operation, although this was a situation not to the liking of the rioters. They hatched a plan to plunge Torquay into darkness by cutting the town's main gas main and a labourer by the name of Chudleigh set off with others for the Livermead area with the intention of fulfilling this aim. Fortunately, the authorities got wind of the plan just in time and, hurrying to the spot, arrested Chudleigh just as he was about to break open the road surface.

117

That was not the end of the fighting and skirmishes between the rioters and the Specials were to continue throughout the night until five o'clock the following morning. Although that marked the end of the riots, the Chief Magistrate held his newly formed force of Specials in reserve for some nights to come in case of any renewed outbreaks. Fortunately for Torquay there were none.

Those who have studied the evolution of the Police Service may have noted that the Devon Constabulary, whilst not in existence at the time of Torquay's first bread riots, had been in existence for some ten years at the time of the second outbreak and therefore was responsible for policing the town. There is, however, no record of any regular police officers being used and, indeed, all the reports confirm that control of the situation was taken by Mr Phillips rather than the local superintendent or Chief Constable. It is only fair to point out, however, that the local establishment of police officers at that time would have been very small and quite incapable of dealing with an event of such magnitude. There are also records which show that, particularly in its early days, the police contingency at Torquay was very inefficient.

Religious Riots

Mention has already been made earlier in this chapter of riots at Honiton involving the activities of the Salvation Army and at Torquay, too, their presence roused opposition in some sections of the public. Once again the 'Devon Weekly News' was at the forefront of reporting the incidents.

It was early May, 1888, when rioting broke out in Torquay and in an article dated 11th May, the 'Devon Weekly News' described how members of the Salvation Army had again marched through the streets of Torquay on a Sunday. This time, however, there was a legal principle at stake and the Army were out to test the strength of the law.

A section of the local Harbour Act stated that "no procession shall take place on a Sunday in any street or public place in the district accompanied by any instrumental music." It was a clause written to prevent the likes of the Salvation Army marching, as they were prone to do, with their brass band to the fore. On the Sunday in question, however, and acting on instructions from their headquarters, the local branch of the Salvation Army intended to test the wording of the Act by splitting their normal march into two parts. The first would comprise only the band and the second the rest of the members. They would then march off in opposite directions thus the band would not be accompanying a procession and the procession would not have a band!

Apparently, their morning procession went off without incident but in the afternoon, anticipating trouble, a crowd estimated at several thousand assembled at the harbour

118

slipway where the Salvationists had assembled for their second open-air meeting of the day. A few minor scuffles broke out and then, at a given signal, the male officers and members of the Army marched off in the direction of Fleet Street. Headed by two flags, they sang as they marched. After a wait of a few minutes the ten members of the band, who had remained at the slipway, struck up and playing at full blast marched off in the opposite direction towards Torbay Road. They were accompanied by Eva Booth, wife of their founder, and Staff Captain McDowall and followed by a large section of the crowd. However a greater number had followed the procession going in the other direction.

Assembly Point: the slipway at Torquay Harbour

At the Torbay Hotel the band turned and started marching in the opposite direction towards the town. At the same time a crowd was coming towards them and soon a general scrimmage was the result. Fortunately, not all those present were hostile towards the band and when a gang from neighbouring Paignton threatened them a crowd of several hundred reportedly leapt to their defence. Their leader, Eva Booth, who was in the front, managed to escape without injury whilst the bandsmen, under the impression that the mob wanted to steal their instruments, held them high above their heads. After some initial apprehensions they formed up again and, instruments playing, marched off followed by the unruly mob. There were also some cheers for the bandsmen. Many were well known local men who had already been convicted of contravening the by-law on processions.

Fortunately, the event did not become a full scale riot, neither were firearms discharged as they were at Honiton. Nevertheless, the authorities took a serious view of the situation and the Torquay Local Board resolved at their next meeting to prosecute Miss Booth and a number of other Salvationists for taking part in a Sunday musical procession.

Dartmouth

At Dartmouth there were problems of a different kind. In 1835 the forces of law and order as we know them today were virtually non-existent except for the military, local militia or, in this case, the coastguard. An event described in a report by the Chief Inspector of Coastguards on the 24th May, following the grounding of the brigantine 'Achor' near Dartmouth, illustrates how such incidents could often bring out the worst in people. In it he graphically states that between five and six hundred people came from all directions and from considerable distances. In their eagerness to plunder the stricken vessel they became violent and, despite the efforts by the coast guard to control the situation and protect the property, most of it was stolen.

Crediton

Finally, as we bring this chapter to a close, early records often show public disorder erupted in many places from time to time. The numbers involved may not be so large, nor may the reasons always be readily identifiable, but the disruption to the local population can be just as aggravating. Crediton provides one such example where a minute to Quarter Sessions in 1855 refers to riots in the town the previous year during which a number of properties were damaged. The reason for the uprising is not known except that, being the era of bread riots elsewhere, it is likely Crediton was affected too. It appears that the Riot Act was read and on this occasion the minute states that a number of local residents were reimbursed a total sum of £8.19s.8d, this money later being recovered by a precept on the local rates.

Chapter Eight

The 19th and 20th CENTURIES

POLICE, PRISON and POLITICAL RIOTS

Totnes Police Riots

It wasn't only the price of bread, or the activities of the Salvation Army, which could provoke a crowd into activity during the 19th century but often it could be the most unlikely of causes. For instance, who would have thought that rioting in support of the local police could occur. Yet it did ... at Totnes.

Although the County Police Act of 1856 gave the Shires the authority to form their own police forces, many boroughs were loath to give up their independent status and sought to retain their own local forces. In fact, some such as Tiverton, managed to keep their independence until World War II even though in Tiverton's case it was the smallest in the country with an establishment of only eleven men, including the Chief Constable. Totnes, however, took a different approach albeit, in the end not a peaceful one.

In 1856 Totnes initially decided against any amalgamation with the newly formed Devon Constabulary and continued to perform successfully until, in 1884, a decision was taken for the local force to be disbanded and the borough to be policed by the county force. By all accounts it was a move which was to prove unpopular with a section of the local towns people as the 'Devon Weekly Times' of the 4th July, 1884, recalls.

According to their report on the Tuesday night, Borough Officers retired from their posts at midnight to make way for officers of the Devon Constabulary. However, about an hour before they did so, around eleven o'clock at night, there were signs of unusual activity in the town. Small bands of men, showing signs of animation, were seen parading the streets whilst other men and women converged in the centre as though waiting for something to happen. By midnight it was estimated that the gatherings had formed a mob some two to three hundred strong. Congregating at the higher end of the High Street they then commenced to parade through the main streets to the Bridgetown area. It was reported that many of them were provided with tin pots and other utensils and were shouting vigorously. Their noise and uproar was described by a local commentator as being 'most hideous'.

The object of their disapproval became abundantly clear when they reached the houses of two or three of the local dignitaries who had sought the amalgamation of the local police with that of the county force. Here they initially voiced their concerns verbally or by groans but it wasn't long before the first stones were thrown. At one of the houses several panes of glass were smashed. The protesters then reached the house of a Mr E. Windeatt who had opposed the move to the new force and here the mood changed with the mob demonstrating their support for him.

For two hours Totnes was in the grip of a riotous assembly although no Riot Act was read. Then, their support in favour of the old borough force well vented, the crowd sang Auld Lang Syne and quietly dispersed out of respect for the departing local constables.

What sparked the opposition to the change in policing is not known but, whatever the reason, it is interesting to speculate what would have happened had the officers from the Devon Constabulary arrived at midnight to pursue their duties at the appointed takeover time. As it was Totnes remained unpoliced throughout the night and for most of the next morning when, at 11.19 a.m., a sergeant and two constables arrived from the Devon Constabulary to take up their posts.

The town's mediaeval guildhall would have been a familiar sight to both local police and residents for it had been used as a courtroom since the 16th Century. Visitors to it today can still see an old prison cell, stocks and a man trap!

The ancient guildhall at Totnes

Prison Riots

With the notorious Dartmoor Prison within the county it is perhaps only natural that one expects a number of stories to emanate from its existence. Situated in the heart of Dartmoor, at Princetown, it indeed has an interesting history. As for Princetown, situated some 1,400 feet above sea level, it was once described as 'a dismal little town built around its prison.' In fairness, despite its above average rainfall and a susceptibility to Dartmoor fog, it is not so dismal these days as tourism has taken over from the prison as its main source of income.

Whilst today one may think that the remoteness of Dartmoor is an ideal spot for a prison, interestingly the reasons for choosing it were more simple than that. It was lobbying on the part of the local landowner, a Sir Thomas Tyrwhitt, who also happened to be friendly with the Prince Regent. At the start of the 19th century the Napoleonic War was in progress and already a large number of French Prisoners had been taken. Many of these were subsequently housed in rotting prison ships moored in the Tamar Estuary at Plymouth and it was this situation which gave Sir Thomas his chance.

Must of his estate included vast tracts of worthless moorland, unsuitable for cultivation or indeed much else. But a prison? He submitted plans for his idea which were accepted and building commenced in 1806. A small town sprang up around the prison and this was named after his friend, the Prince Regent, Princetown! The building was completed in 1809 at a cost of £130,000 and soon the inmates were transferred from the prison ships and joined by other French prisoners. The Latin inscription above the main gate, when translated, reads "Spare the Vanquished," and not "Abandon hope all ye who enter here" as is popularly believed. However, the latter may have been more appropriate!

By 1813 the prison population had grown to over eight thousand when American seamen captured during the 1812-14 Anglo-American War joined the French prisoners. Christmas 1814 saw peace declared with the Americans but then a dispute arose as to who should pay for the repatriation of the American prisoners. Neither side would agree and as a result the prisoners remained at Princetown. It was a situation which was to give rise to one of the prison's ugliest incidents.

Not surprisingly, the American inmates became increasingly restless at their continued detention and it was then that a comparatively minor incident in the exercise yard became blown out of all proportion. In an over-reaction the Governor called out the military and ordered them to fire on the prisoners in the yard. Seven prisoners were killed and over fifty seriously injured. It has been said that the casualties would have been very much greater had it not been for the compassion of many of the troops who could not bear to fire on unarmed men and fired into the air instead. To give some idea of the prisoners' grievances, the conditions within the prison were such that a further two hundred and eleven Americans were to die there from a mixture of disease, deprivation and the penetrating Dartmoor winter cold.

In many ways the parish church at Princetown stands as a reminder of those brutal days for it was built between the years of 1810-1815 by American and French prisoners. Many have their final resting place within the prison cemetery. It is one of the more unusual links we have with the United States, albeit a sad one. Nevertheless, it is this historical connection which brings many American tourists each year to Princetown and its church.

At the end of the wars came the repatriation of prisoners and the need for the prison diminished. However, its fortunes were to change in 1850 when the decision was taken to turn it into a convict prison, a role which still continues today. During the next century and a half there have been many more disturbances at Dartmoor but all, bar one, have been dealt with successfully by the prison authorities. The exception came in January 1932.

Unrest had been simmering for a number of weeks, the main grievance being the state of the prison food. On Sunday the men assembled as usual for the morning church service in the prison chapel only on this occasion the Governor decided to address them. There was instant booing and he was forced to step down, only the timely intervention of the prison chaplain saving the day. However, the seeds for an uprising had been sown.

The following morning, whilst being once again marched to the chapel, the prisoners rebelled. Now they were ready for action. Secretly they had been making weapons in the prison workshops whilst others had purloined pick handles, crowbars and spades which were used for work within the prison quarry. A mutiny had begun. Much blood would be spilled and damage done.

The mob were now in full cry and, in force, marched to the administration block where they demanded the release of all prisoners held in the punishment block and threatened to burn down the prison if their demands were not met. Visiting the prison at the time was an Assistant Prison Commissioner from London and he was immediately attacked. Only the efforts of one of the prisoners saved him from possible death, an act which subsequently led to a reduction in the prisoner's sentence.

The situation was deteriorating rapidly. The prisoners had occupied the Governor's and other offices, looting and setting fire to effects as they went. And just to make sure their efforts at arson were not thwarted, they also destroyed the prison's fire engine! However, by now the warders were beginning to get organised. Armed, they assumed positions on top of the walls around the prison although at this stage there appeared to be no attempt by the prisoners to make a mass breakout. They still seemed content to continue their wave of destruction within the prison itself. However, when a couple of prisoners had climbed onto the roof of the twine shed they were immediately shot by the warders and this could have been the reason for their reluctance to charge the walls.

The end of the mutiny has been described by some as an anticlimax. Police were quickly mobilised by the County Constabulary and also from the neighbouring City of Plymouth force. The military also arrived in some force although they were kept in reserve as the police contingent charged through the prison gates. Truncheons drawn, the officers showed little mercy to the rioting prisoners and many skulls were cracked as the inmates retreated back to their cells. Had this swift police operation not been successful no doubt casualties would have been high. The hundred armed troops standing-by outside would have immediately been deployed, ready to open fire if necessary. As it was a number of prisoners received minor injuries as a result of the baton charge but none of the police were hurt. The warders had not been so lucky for during the rioting a number had been injured, one so seriously that he was invalided out of the service.

The conclusion to this notable episode in the prison's history came in April 1932 when a special sitting of the Court of Assize was convened at Exeter and thirty-three prisoners were arraigned before the Judge. Charges ranged from attempted murder, causing bodily harm and rioting to causing wilful damage. Eleven prisoners were found 'not guilty' and acquitted. The other twenty-two were not so fortunate. Their sentences ranged from a comparatively light additional six months imprisonment, added to their existing sentences, to ten years penal servitude.

The prison still appears as bleak as ever but changes have been made. At one time only the most hardened criminals would be sent there, the majority serving life sentences for murder or other serious crimes. Prison breaks were few but when they occurred the searches were so intensive that few ever escaped the moor and most were glad to be recaptured. The legends surrounding Dartmoor's notorious bogs was another factor which put fear into the hearts of many would be escapees. However, the erection of a giant TV mast at Princetown around the 1960's changed matters. Its warning lights for aircraft could be seen for miles and for the first time escaping prisoners had a reference point. The old problem of 'going around in circles' no longer existed. Prison reforms also affected Dartmoor and gradually its status was downgraded. It is no longer a high security prison and today its inmates are no better or worse than will be found elsewhere.

A view towards the main gates of Dartmoor Prison

Political Riots

The punch thrown by the Deputy Prime Minister which almost floored a protester during Britain's 2001 General Election Campaign almost pales into insignificance when compared with events of a century ago. The only difference being that today TV pictures of such incidents can be instantly flashed around the world whereas in days gone by there was only the local press account.

In this chapter it is their reports which today give an insight into the political violence which appears to have once been almost a common occurrence. Many places were affected at one time or another and Exmouth, Newton Abbot and Ashburton are three Devon towns which happened to be reported upon.

Exmouth

Bread and military riots were not the only source of problems at Exmouth. Towards the end of the 19th Century, and indeed into the 20th, political agitation was quite common and often the simplest of matters could quickly inflame a crowd. The following incident which occurred in Exmouth on the 13th July, 1892, during the course of a general election, illustrates this only too well. Its implications were no doubt much greater than its instigator could have possibly imagined at the time.

Details of the event which led to rioting during the during the 1892 election actually arose out of a common practice. Again we have to thank the late Bill Gorfin, a great Exmothian and editor of the 'Exmouth Journal' from 1909 to 1964, for details. He was a youngster at the time and recollected that during the election Sir John Kennaway, for the Tories, beat the Liberal candidate, a Dr. Aubret, for a seat in the House. The election itself seemed relatively trouble free but the situation rapidly deteriorated when a coachman, sporting the blue rosette of the Tory party, put the whip behind his coach to scare off two boys who were riding on the back axles.

Although it was a common occurrence for youngsters to hitch illicit rides in this way and for coachmen to react accordingly, on this occasion it happened the lads were wearing the yellow rosettes of the Liberals. Immediately some observers deemed it to be an act of 'Tory Tyranny' and it did not take long for the word to spread and passions became quickly aroused.

During the rest of the day the situation deteriorated even further and that evening a number of Conservatives were forced to take refuge in the town's London Hotel, barricading the doors against the mob which had formed outside. Even so the glass panes of the doors were broken before the local police superintendent arrived at the scene with four constables. Then, seeing the state of the crowd, he immediately sent for a further eleven men who were being held in reserve at the police station. The mob then turned its attention to the officers, hurling stones at them. One, a Constable Beer, was reportedly hit on the chest by a brick and badly injured.

By eleven o'clock at night the disorder and violence had increased to such an extent that an order was given for the police to draw truncheons and charge. This had the effect of breaking the mob up into smaller factions and for these to disperse and cause problems elsewhere. By midnight matters were so bad that a local magistrate, a Captain Luke, was summoned to the scene and asked to read the Riot Act. He addressed the unruly mob but refused to do more. Without the force of the Riot Act to back him the superintendent withdrew his men to the police station. It was to be a painful withdrawal for the officers came under heavy pelting with stones and it was reported that every one of them was hit.

Twenty-one men were ultimately summoned for their part in the affray and even their subsequent hearing in the Public Hall was not without further incident. Many of their supporters had to be ejected for barracking. As for Captain Luke who had refused to read the Riot Act, he had died in the meanwhile so could not give evidence. On a technical point, the fact that the police had used their truncheons before the Riot Act had been read, meant all the defendants were acquitted!

Newton Abbot

Serious rioting occurred in Newton Abbot on the 18th January, 1908, following the result of a local parliamentary by-election. At the core of the problem was the shock defeat of the Liberal candidate, a Mr. C. R. Buxton, in a constituency which had long been a stronghold for the party.

Newton Abbot, situated within the Mid-Devon or Ashburton Parliamentary Constituency, was an area where Liberal policies of 'free trade' greatly appealed to the voters who mainly relied on agriculture for their living. Their sitting Liberal M.P., Mr. H.T. Eve, was popular with the voters and seemed well established. In 1907, however, he was promoted to become a Judge of the High Court, an appointment which inevitably meant he had to vacate his seat in Parliament. A by-election was called and the two main parties prepared for the contest. The Conservative candidate was a Captain Morrison-Bell whilst Mr C.R. Buxton was to fight the Liberal cause. On paper the latter was set for an easy win.

However, nothing is certain and right from the outset feelings began to run high. There were signs that this was not going to be an easy election and in its run-up there were frequent reports of skirmishes between supporters of the rival parties. Pre-election meetings also proved to be often disorderly affairs with violence frequently erupting. Without recourse to the media which modern politicians enjoy, television was not yet invented and radio was still in its infancy, posters played a great part in any election fight and frequently portrayed opponents in an unsavory light although, on reflection, this is a tactic little changed today! In Newton Abbot the Conservatives produced large posters portraying Mr. Buxton as a 'carpetbagger'.

There was, however, another player in this contest who came in on the side of the Conservatives ... Emmeline Pankhurst. Mrs Pankhurst's main role as the country's leading suffragette was of course to campaign for 'votes for women' and she arrived at Newton Abbot with her daughter, Sylvia, and a fellow suffragette, a Mrs Martell. In pursuing their own cause they allied themselves to Captain Morrison-Bell and the Conservative party. Finally, all the campaigning was over and votes had been cast. All that was left was to await the result.

By one of those quirks of fate both main parties had located their clubs in the same street, Newton Abbot's Union Street. Furthermore, they were almost opposite each other. It was not surprising, therefore, that on the morning of the 18th January, 1908, as the declaration of the result was awaited, Union Street was thronged with supporters from both sides. It was reported that the red, white and blue rosettes worn by the Conservative supporters were greatly outnumbered by the red and yellow colours of the Liberal party. Shortly after noon the result came through. Morrison-Bell, the Conservative, had been elected by a majority of 559. It was a devastating result for the Liberals.

Liberal supporters became angry and emotions ran high. The sudden appearance of Mrs Pankhurst, her daughter and Mrs Martell was the catalyst they needed. Here were the outsiders who had dared to come to Newton Abbot to support the Conservative cause. It was time to take revenge. The mob made a move towards the three women who started to run, pursued by the angry crowd. The women managed to reach the doorway of Banbury's grocer's shop where they attempted to hold the mob at bay with their umbrellas until Mr Banbury, seeing their plight, let them into the shop and sheltered them in an upstairs room.

By now a contingent of police had arrived under the command of a Superintendent Roberts. They, too, met the wrath of the hostile crowd who pelted them with rotten eggs and tore the tunic from the back of the Superintendent. A contemporary report states that several of the police were struck down and a number received serious injuries.

The angry mob was still intent on reaching the suffragettes and newspaper reports said that their intentions were to throw the women into the River Lemon which flowed through the town and were making these known through a series of fear provoking chants.

Sensing their extreme danger if they stayed where they were, a Harry Balls arrived on the scene. He was the owner of the town's first garage and brought with him a brand new 10-hp Darracq car to help in a rescue attempt.

The attempt succeeded but not without much further fighting during which it is said that Mrs Pankhurst took an active part before being knocked down and trampled on by the angry crowd. Eventually the police were able to tumble the three women into the comparative safety of the Darracq, by which time they were described as 'injured and disheveled'. As Mr. Balls drove slowly from the scene the police secured the car by providing two constables on each running board, one on the bonnet and another on the back, plus the addition of a line of constables on foot at either side. That was not quite the end for it was also reported that the vehicle ran into further trouble whilst being driven through Kingsteignton before finally making the safety of the women's hotel at Teignmouth.

Meanwhile, back in Union Street, the mob had turned their attention to the Conservative Club which they were attacking with stones and any other missiles they could find. Virtually every pane of glass in the building was shattered. To be seen wearing a red, white and blue rosette was to make one an immediate target for attack and one farmer, displaying his party's colours, was dragged from his horse, attacked and rolled in the mud.

By then events were so much out of control that the Chief Constable arrived at the scene in person. He came mounted on a horse with a small contingent of mounted police officers behind him. In addition there were some one hundred officers on foot. A police escort brought two Magistrates to the scene with the intention that they should read the Riot Act but when they saw the large number of women and children in the crowd they refused to do so out of fear that they may be injured in any police reaction. With the Magistrates returning home and the Riot Act unread, the police formed up in close ranks and, although the immediate target for missile throwers, were forbidden to take any effective action to disperse the crowd and restore order.

Until then most of the rioting had taken place in daylight but as darkness fell the situation became even worse. Again eye witness reports say that the mob was in complete control whilst the large police contingent obeyed their orders and stood passively by. Just when it seemed there was no solution in sight the end came in quick, dramatic fashion.

Midnight had just passed and with the hands of the clock slowly ticking towards one o'clock the mob was still in full cry. Suddenly, one of the policemen was brought heavily to the ground. It was a decisive moment for the incident was to provoke a police reaction after being passive for so long. The police ranks surged forward into the crowd, no longer afraid to use force. Within minutes the mob, sensing a change in tactics, broke up and quietly slunk away to their homes. Some said the police should have taken firm action whilst others praised their tolerance under such circumstances.

When Newton Abbot took stock the following day there had been much damage and many people, not least the police, had been injured, some seriously. One who paid the ultimate price for an evening of folly was a Sergeant Rendell. His body was recovered from the Bradley Mill leat which runs through the western side of the town but the circumstances under which he died remains a mystery. It is known however that he was a staunch supporter of the Conservatives.

Above: The Conservative Club in Union Street which was erected as the Mid Devon Constitutional Club in 1887

Bradley Mill Leat where Sergeant Rendell's body was discovered

The local newspaper, the 'Flying Post' reported the incident on the 25th January, 1908, in the following words:

> *"Sinister rumours became current when it was known that Sergeant Rendell, 65 years, late of the Royal Marines, and an ardent Unionist, had been found dead in the Bradley Mill Leat on Sunday morning. There was a severe blow over one eye ..."*

At the subsequent inquest on Sergeant Rendell evidence was given by a number of friends that he was a man of sober habits but had been drinking on the night. Medical evidence was also given to the effect that the blow, although serious, was not the cause of death. That had been drowning. In the absence of any further evidence as to the cause of his injuries a verdict of 'Found Drowned' was recorded.

Needless to say the rumours of foul play did not desist!

Ashburton

Although the 1908 riot at Newton Abbot occurred within the Ashburton parliamentary constituency, Ashburton itself was not significantly involved on that occasion although it had a history of political violence.

During the first half of the 19th Century it was the town's Golden Lion Hotel which seemed to be at the centre of dubious electoral activities. One which has been the subject of comment occurred around 1825 when a William Baron took up occupancy of the hotel. He was described as a 'die-hard Tory'. It also seems he developed his own method of persuading the local townsfolk to join his particular political cause. This he achieved by hiring the more unsavory characters in the community to 'advise' the others on how they should vote or at least to abstain.

It seems, however that matters came to a head during an election held in 1837. The account of the incident is rather sketchy but it appears that one of Baron's 'hirelings' went one stage further than usual and actually kidnapped one of the town's leading Liberals. This provoked an immediate reaction in the town and what was described as 'full-scale rioting' broke out.

The Golden Lion, Ashburton, in 2001

Interestingly, the Golden Lion continued to play a part in politics up until the end of the 20th century and in fact became the venue for the annual conference of one of our most recognisable political parties .... The Monster Raving Loony Party. The late landlord was one of their leading members, becoming their first political success when he was elected Ashburton's mayor!

However, the inn's chequered political past it is unlikely to be repeated in the future. As this book goes to print major renovation work is being undertaken to convert it to residential accommodation. Luckily for the amateur historian it seems likely its name will be retained by merely substituting 'House' for 'Hotel'.

THE EPILOGUE

Looking back over past the past two millennia one sees that Devon has had its share of Battles, Bullets and Mayhem, both in a military and civil sense. Arguably, our greatest "battle" was the Second World War and although a half a century has passed since it ended there are still many for whom it is a fresh memory. Furthermore, so many books have been written about this crucial period in our history it was not felt prudent to dwell upon it in this book.

For those who seek reminders, however, there are many to be found. Remains can be found of former wartime airfields, there are the odd pillboxes in fields and, of course, most towns and villages will have their memorials to servicemen who fell in battle. Of these, there is perhaps none finer that that of the Royal Navy on Plymouth Hoe or to lost aircrew, both British and Allied, which stands nearby.

However, to end this book it was felt that for many there is probably no better reminder of suffering in time of war than the ruined shell of Charles Church, Plymouth. Of 17th Century origins it was badly damaged during the Nazi blitzes of 1941-42. If was a period when countless ordinary members of communities throughout Devon and elsewhere also lost their lives.

Fortunately, we have not seen the like of it since.

Long may the peace continue.